W9-CDF-526

Things to Do When You Turn 60

What the Press wrote about
Fifty Things To Do When You Turn Fifty

"A collection of essays that are helpful, humorous, and encouraging . . . could cause the market for black balloons to collapse!"

Atlanta Journal Constitution

"It's a great book to browse or read piecemeal. Highly recommended; sales of the book will be donated to cancer organizations."

Library Journal

"It gives advice and tips about taking stock, taking action, or taking a break."

Newsday

"This book is worth a thumb-through because it's fun and a quick read — and that's a plus because, as author Erica Jong points out in her essay, 50 is the time when time itself begins to seem short."

St. Louis Post-Dispatch

"Those who want reassurance that 50 is the age at which you start reaping the benefits of your labors will find much to appreciate here."

Publishers Weekly

"An upbeat answer to the over-the-hill gang."

Miami Herald

MAKING THE MOST OF YOUR MILESTONE BIRTHDAY

SECOND EDITION

Things to Do When You Turn 60

Edited by Ronnie Sellers

Commissioning Editors Sheri Bell-Rehwoldt
Joy Darlington • Bruce Fraser
General Editor Andrea Feld

Copyright © 2018 Sellers Publishing, Inc.
All rights reserved.

Sellers Publishing, Inc.
161 John Roberts Road, South Portland, Maine 04106
Visit our Web site: www.sellerspublishing.com
E-mail: rsp@rsvp.com

Ronnie Sellers: President and Publisher
Mary Baldwin: Managing Editor
Charlotte Cromwell: Production Editor

The following essays are reprinted with permission of the publishers: *Go to where the art is* (p. 107) is an excerpt from *We Flew Over The Bridge: Performance Art, Story Quilts, and Tar Beach* by Faith Ringgold, © 2005 Duke University Press, and is reprinted with permission. *Rediscover yourself at 60* (p. 293) is an excerpt from *Moving Beyond Words* by Gloria Steinem, copyright © 1994 by Gloria Steinem and is reprinted with permission from Simon & Schuster Adult Publishing Group. *Credits continued on page 375.*

ISBN 13: 978-1-4162-4661-9
Library of Congress Control Number: 2018932511

No portion of this book may be reproduced, stored in a retrieval system, or transmitted in any form or by any means, mechanical, electronic, photocopying, recording, or otherwise, without the written permission of the publisher.

Printed and bound in United States of America.

Contents

Introduction

Turning 60 isn't what it used to be. Turning 60 is definitely much easier now than it was even a generation ago. The reason for this is obvious; people are turning 60 at a much younger age than they used to. My children tell me that I say this only because I have already turned sixty, but (as usual) I know better. I am right about this. Sixty is *young*, and there are 78 million others turning 60 who will back me up.

I'm guessing that you are one of them. You wouldn't be reading this book if you weren't. When you look in the mirror, do you see an old person looking back at you? No way. You see yourself. Sure, you might have thinner hair and a few more wrinkles than you had when you were 30, but you are still basically the same person you've always known and loved. You are in decent shape. You have lapses in memory once in awhile, but you still manage to find your way home every night. And besides, there are so many people . . . including scores of famous, sexy, attractive people, who are older than you are. What have you got to worry about?

Think about it. If you want to celebrate your 60th birthday by going to a rock concert, you can pony up $500 for a ticket and go see the English band that made "Time Is On My Side" a hit half a centuty ago. As you sip your mineral water and listen to them perform through your sound-dampening earplugs, you *can* get satisfaction . . . from the knowledge that you are younger than the gnarly musicians prancing around on the stage in front of you.

You should be upbeat about turning 60 because so many good things seem to happen when you reach that milestone. It's as if you receive some kind of papal — or presidential — dispensation and most of your sins are forgiven. For instance, when former president George Walker Bush turned 60, he jumped up onto a podium in front of a large crowd and announced joyously, "This year, two of my father's favorite people turned 60; me and Bill Clinton." Bill Clinton, the man who denied George Bush Senior a second term in the Oval Office, became one of that elder stateman's favorite people. If that's not proof that amazing things can happen to you when you turn 60, I don't know what is.

Let's be honest, we all know that things have changed. When we were younger, people who were 60 were geezers who were counting the minutes until they had to check in to nursing homes. We treated them with the courtesy and respect they were due (which is more than can be said, by the way, for the way kids treat 60-year-olds these days). We gave them our seats on crowded buses and we kept a close eye on them at intersections to make sure they didn't need help walking across the street. Beyond that, for the most part, we ignored them. We also disregarded almost everything they said. They were 60, after all, too old to be worth listening to. We were children of the new era, much too unique . . . too gifted and talented . . . too predestined to fame and fortune to need advice from senior citizens. We were the ones whose mission it was to change the world. They were the ones who had screwed up the world in the first place.

There was no way that anyone over 60 could ever understand anything about our younger generation because there had never been a generation as special as ours. And we're still special. And that's why we're younger at 60 than anyone has ever been before . . . and better looking, too. And the facts support this.

If you look at the National Vital Statistics Reports for the United States through the last 80 years, the data proves beyond question that 60-year-olds used to be much older than we are. Incredible as this might seem, in 1930 the life expectancy for a newborn white male in the United States was only 60 years (64 years for a white female . . . 47 years and 49 years for an African-American male and female respectively). So in the past, when you turned 60, you were more than just an old person, you were a walking miracle. You had made it through 60 seasons without getting written out of the script. Still, there was little comfort in that, especially if you stopped to count how few original cast members were left standing there with you. You knew that at age 60, the final act was well under way.

Today, for most of us, turning 60 merely means that we've reached the intermission; the end of the fifth inning; the 16-mile marker in the 26-mile race. We still have a long way to go, and anything could happen before we cross the finish line. Because we are turning 60 at such a young age, we are able to look to the future with optimism and enthusiasm. If we manage our finances properly, the best years of our lives will be those that are ahead of us. And therein lies the rub. If we don't manage our finances properly, turning 60 at a young age could mean many years of riding a bicycle to and from a job at Burger King.

And that's where this book, *60 Things To Do When You Turn 60,* comes in. The celebrities, artists, pundits, financial wizards, medical specialists, and theologians who were kind enough to contribute to it provide a wealth of information for those approaching their Big Six-Oh. When taken in its entirety, this book comprises a veritable instruction manual on how to enjoy the process . . . and it is a process . . . of turning 60. Perhaps even more valuable is the expert advice offered by contributors about things to do afterward to make the years that follow as fulfilling and rewarding as possible.

So if you are one of the 13,680 youthful North Americans who will turn 60 every day (570 per hour!) through the next 10 years, I recommend that you pull up a comfortable chair, relax, and settle in with this book. It will make you laugh. It may bring tears to your eyes. It could even be the impetus for change. But most importantly, it will enable you to appreciate how fortunate you are to be one of the youngest 60-year-olds ever.

Ronnie Sellers

Section One

GET BACK

(The Beatles, 1969)

Never, ever give up

Be bold, be fearless, and chase your dream
no matter how old you are.

by Diana Nyad

25 million people worldwide rooted for Diana Nyad as she approached the Florida shore, at long last achieving her 35-year-old dream of becoming the first person to swim from Cuba to Florida.

Diana is not one to quit. On her fifth attempt, speaking the words "Never Ever Give Up" to the wildly cheering crowd on a Key West beach on September 2, 2013, Diana may have been dazed and physically spent, but she showed the world what persistence and bold spirit can manifest.

Diana stroked the amazing 110.86 miles in 52 hours, 54 minutes, 18 seconds.

A worldwide response of inspiration came flooding toward Diana, from personal messages from President Obama and Hillary Clinton to literally millions of people who felt their own lives lifted with Diana's "Find a Way" philosophy.

Daring to reach for the stars, this swim beginning to seem impossible (after her four attempts over 35 years and other strong swimmers trying and failing since 1950), Diana has motivated the world at large to live fearlessly, to chase one's dreams with unwavering commitment.

The second statement the victorious 64-year-old made on that Key West beach? "You're never too old to chase your dreams." And her third statement on that historic day: "It looks a solitary sport, but it's a TEAM."

Courage, bold vision, and the ability to articulate her life philosophies have propelled Diana through an inspiring life.

A prominent sports journalist, filing for National Public Radio, ABC's Wide World of Sports, The New York Times, the Huffington Post and others, Diana has carved her place as one of our compelling storytellers.

Her memoir, *Find a Way*, has earned worldwide praise. She has written three other books and speaks French and Spanish fluently.

Diana has also earned the reputation of a uniquely entertaining and inspiring public speaker and has taken her one-woman stage show "ONWARD!" to a theatrical performance.

Diana and her Cuba Swim Head Handler Bonnie Stoll have launched an initiative called EverWalk, to lead us walking along the epic outdoor corridors of America. Diana and Bonnie intend to turn us into a nation of millions of walkers.

And then there are the crises. Of course there are. And the vomiting starts, the seawater, you're not well, you're wearing a jellyfish mask for the ultimate protection. It's difficult to swim in. It's causing abrasions on the inside of the mouth, but the tentacles can't get you.

And the hypothermia sets in. The water's 85 degrees, and yet you're losing weight and using calories, and as you come over toward the side of the boat, not allowed to touch it, not allowed to get out, but Bonnie and her team hand me nutrition and asks me what I'm doing, am I all right, I am seeing the Taj Mahal over here. I'm in a very different state, and I'm thinking, wow, I never thought I'd be running into the Taj Mahal out here. It's gorgeous. I mean, how long did it take them to build that? It's just — So, uh, wooo.

And then we kind of have a cardinal rule that I'm never told, really, how far it is, because we don't know how far it is. What's going to happen to you between this point and that point? What's going to happen to the weather and the currents and, God forbid, you're stung when you don't think you could be stung in all this armor, and Bonnie made a decision coming into that third morning that I was suffering and I was hanging on by a thread and she said, "Come here," and I came close to the boat, and she said, "Look, look out there," and I saw light, because the day's easier than the night, and I thought we were coming into day, and I saw a stream of white light along the horizon, and I said, "It's going to be morning soon." And she said, "No, those are the lights of Key West." It was 15 more hours, which for most swimmers would be a long time. You have no idea how many 15-hour training swims I had done.

So here we go, and I somehow, without a decision, went into no counting of strokes and no singing and no quoting Stephen Hawking and the parameters of the universe, I just went into thinking about this dream, and why, and how.

And as I said, when I turned 60, it wasn't about that concrete "Can you do it?" That's the everyday machinations. That's the discipline, and it's the preparation, and there's a pride in that.

But I decided to think, as I went along about the phrase usually is reaching for the stars, and in my case, it's reaching for the horizon. And when you reach for the horizon, as I've proven, you may not get there, but what a tremendous build of character and spirit that you lay down. What a foundation you lay down in reaching for those horizons.

And now the shore is coming, and there's just a little part of me that's sad. The epic journey is going to be over.

So many people come up to me now and say, "What's next? We love that! That little tracker that was on the computer? When are you going to do the next one? We just can't wait to follow the next one." Well, they were just there for 53 hours, and I was there for years. And so there won't be another epic journey in the ocean.

But the point is, and the point was that every day of our lives is epic, and I'll tell you, when I walked up onto that beach, staggered up onto that beach, and I had so many times in a very puffed up ego way, rehearsed what I would say on the beach. When Bonnie thought that the back of my throat was swelling up, and she brought the medical team over to our boat to say that she's really beginning to have trouble breathing. Another 12, 24 hours in the saltwater, the whole thing — and I just thought in my hallucinatory moment, that I heard the word tracheotomy.

And Bonnie said to the doctor, "I'm not worried about her not breathing. If she can't talk when she gets to the shore, she's going to be pissed off."

But the truth is, all those orations that I had practiced just to get myself through some training swims as motivation, it wasn't like that. It was a very real moment with that crowd, with my team. We did it. I didn't do it. We did it. And we'll never forget it. It'll always be part of us. And the three things that I did sort of blurt out when we got there, was first, "Never, ever give up." I live it. What's the phrase from today from Socrates? To be is to do. So I don't stand up and say, don't ever give up. I didn't give up, and there was action behind these words.

The second is, "You can chase your dreams at any age; you're never too old." Sixty-four, that no one at any age, any gender, could ever do, has done it, and there's no doubt in my mind that I am at the prime of my life today.

Yeah. Thank you.

And the third thing I said on that beach was, "It looks like the most solitary endeavor in the world, and in many ways, of course, it is, and in other ways, and the most important ways, it's a team, and if you think I'm a badass, you want to meet Bonnie."

Bonnie, where are you? Where are you? There's Bonnie Stoll. My buddy.

The Henry David Thoreau quote goes, "When you achieve your dreams, it's not so much what you get as who you have become in achieving them." And yeah, I stand before you now. In the three months since that swim ended, I've sat down with Oprah and I've been in President Obama's Oval Office. I've been invited to speak in front of esteemed groups. I've signed a wonderful major book contract. All of that's great, and I don't denigrate it. I'm proud of it all, but the truth is, I'm walking around tall because I am that bold, fearless person, and I will be every day, until it's time for these days to be done.

Thank you. Thank you. Thank you. Thank you. Thank you. Thank you. Thank you. Thank you. Find a way!

Originally published as *"Never, Ever Give Up,"* in *The Singju Post Staff,* November 29, 2014.

2

Take off your clothes

When you are 60, of course you can wear purple — or else nothing at all!

by Cynthia Thayer

Novelist Cynthia Thayer is the author of *Strong for Potatoes, A Certain Slant of Light, Indigo Tide* and *A Brief Lunacy*. She has taught fiction writing at workshops in Maine. She spins yarns of all kinds and dyes them with indigo and madder from her garden, and lives with her family on their coastal organic farm in Downeast Maine.

When I turned 60, I threw a big party with a live jazz band and lots of great dancing, and I knit myself a very long indigo sweater because I wanted something warm between my ass and a cold seat. But the best thing I did, with my yarn spinning group, was to produce a calendar filled from cover to cover with naked women and multicolored yarns in a celebration of the "art of handspinning and the ageless beauty of women."

I've heard it said that when we turn 60, we won't care what other people think, perhaps because our parents will be either dead or too old to care what we do. That's not quite true. We still care, but the emphasis has changed from coworkers who are competing with us for seniority and responsibility because we're trying to get to the top of the ladder and that next-door neighbor who thinks our lawn is too straggly to friends we choose to be involved with.

Our spinning group gathers every Wednesday at someone's house laden with cookies and pickled beans and spinning wheels and bags of colored carded fleece to spin. During our yearly retreat, we were lounging in a hot tub sipping wine, discussing wool, breeds of sheep, dyeing silk, the state of the world, and getting old, when my friend Susanne came up with the zany idea of producing a naked spinners calendar, replete with soup recipes and hints for choosing a fleece and filled with glorious socks and sweaters, to help finance our trip to Ireland. As our plans developed, we decided to donate a percentage of the money we made to breast cancer research. We threw ourselves into this project that ultimately transformed our lives.

Our first session began with a glass of merlot and great hesitancy on the part of some. Our last only needed a shout of "everybody ready?" to begin a ceremonial tossing of all manner of clothing out of the camera's range amidst sounds of laughter.

Thirty women living on the rugged coast of Maine decided to take the leap. Doug, a photographer friend, took pictures of us walking hand in hand across a field, our assorted bottoms peeking out from beneath blue and purple and green colored patterns of handspun, handknit sweaters. Another picture featured nine naked women, fanned out, prostrate on the grass, our glorious socks touching, our bare bums forming a dazzling array. One in our midst wanted to do the shot but didn't want to disrobe. I believe it was at that moment when we said, "Oh, please, join us; sure, wear your clothes," that I felt I had arrived at a point that I would care only what people I loved and respected thought of me.

We continued doing "shoots" of shearing sheep on a nearby island and slogging our spinning wheels through a mud-rutted woods road, naked and loving it. We spun en masse at the edge of the sea from baskets of fleece, our wheels perched on rocks and seaweed-strewn sand, our fingers silky smooth from the lanolin. Striped knee-high socks, a magenta angora hat, and sturdy rugs dyed with indigo and goldenrod from our gardens enhanced the rugged Maine coast and the *au naturel* women of the Wednesday Spinners. We knit in a line on our porch from baskets of brightly dyed yarns and piled into our horsedrawn sleigh buck-naked on a snowy December day.

We were featured on CNN, in *The Sun* and the *New York Daily News*, on FOX news and even Japanese radio. We sold almost 20,000 copies of the calendar, and letters poured in from all over the world praising our courage and spirit. And yes, we did go to Ireland.

Sure, it's easy to take off your clothes when you're young and confident with perfect skin and a size ten body. And then there are those years in between when it can be dreadfully difficult. But when you're 60 or 70 and covered with sags and wrinkles and scars and rolls, it becomes easy again when you're with people who cherish your ideas and your beauty, both inner and outer.

No, we don't reflect the American standard of what women are supposed to look like. But who does? A few select models? The Hollywood elite? We are who we are. We are a group of women who love spinning wool, knitting, weaving, crocheting, and ourselves. We are crones. We are the wise ones. If we happen to be spinning on one of the offshore islands and the weather is hot, we throw off our clothes with abandon and include one or two who have waded in with shorts and a T-shirt in our laughter and our splashing. We have learned to be different. And we don't care what other people think, except for those whom we respect.

Sixty is a time for wearing purples and greens together, for shaving our heads if we want to, for spinning madder red yarns full of gold threads, for knitting a sweater that hangs down to our knees, for laughing 'til our sides ache, for spreading our love of being different to the younger generation, for frolicking in the waves with our friends until our skin is numb, for creating our own triathlons, for hiring a rock band and boogying 'til we drop. It's a time to change professions or paint our toenails ten different colors.

And 60 is a time of surrounding ourselves with friends who will love us whether we make fools of ourselves or wear clothes that don't match or fail at our latest creative project. It is also a time for showing our grandchildren and the children of the world that it is good to follow the road less traveled, the one that's grassy and wants wear, and that we will love them and support them on their journey.

3

Let it go

Don't let unpleasant memories bog you down. This release technique is safe and requires no more than the skill of tapping your hands and feet!

by Daniel J. Benor, M.D.

Daniel J. Benor, M.D., is a wholistic psychiatric psychotherapist who includes bodymind approaches, spiritual awareness, and healing in his practice. Dr. Benor is the author of *Healing Research, Volumes I–IV* and many articles on wholistic, spiritual healing. He appears internationally on radio and TV and is the editor and producer of the *International Journal of Healing and Caring — On-Line* at www.ijhc.org. His website is www.danielbenor.com.com.

I imagine that, as you reach 60, you've experienced a thing or two that was traumatic. Am I right? Perhaps you've even experienced several traumatic events. And though the offending event may be long behind you, you may still feel upset about it. But the good news is, those feelings you associate with a trauma can be released. The technique is simple and something I share with my clients regularly.

I developed my technique based on two tools that I had previously used in my practice. These tools are called Eye Movement Desensitization and Reprocessing (EMDR) and Emotional Freedom Technique (EFT). EMDR uses eye movements and other outside stimuli to help the client sort through negative feelings and sensations that may well up when remembering a trauma, while EFT uses positive affirmations to replace negative thoughts.

Each one has pros and cons. EMDR is well supported by research, but it can evoke strong emotional releases and should be practiced with a therapist. On the other hand, EFT is safe and can be used for self-healing, but less research has been done and therefore it is less supported in the psychotherapy field.

My technique combines the best of both tools. I call it WHEE, Wholistic Hybrid derived from EMDR and EFT. It grew out of my own professional and personal journey.

When I learned about psychotherapy as a teenager, I knew it was what I wanted to do. I couldn't imagine anyone actually getting paid to do something so fascinating! I studied psychology as an undergraduate before going to medical school. I trained as a psychiatrist in an era when psychiatry was mostly psychotherapy. But as the years wore on, managed care forced many psychiatrists to stop spending a full hour helping clients. Instead we are expected to do our work in 15- to 20-minute "medication management" visits. I constantly sought to develop ways of providing psychotherapy along with the medications but was unable within my limited time-frame to use the slow, psychodynamic approaches I was taught as a psychiatric resident.

During these same years, I also developed an interest in spiritual awareness and healing — topics that had never been mentioned in my psychology, medicine, or psychiatry training. As I discussed this interest with colleagues and clients, I learned that for many people, spirituality is confined to their place of worship, and they say that in this context their experience of spirituality (such as it is) is not particularly moving or satisfying. They find more restriction within their religion than inspiration and enhancement.

My personal awakening to spirituality developed through a gradual series of experiences. Some of my practices are more widely recognized as spiritual in nature, such as hatha yoga and meditation. Other practices, less so: I consider being a psychotherapist, healer, lecturer, and workshop leader a spiritual endeavor because I learn from clients and students who synchronistically often teach me as much as I teach them.

My current beliefs in spirituality are clear enough and strong enough that I feel confident in sharing them with others — in my practice, in experiential workshops, and in my writing. Many of my lessons in healing, both psychological and spiritual, are encapsulated in WHEE. You don't need any special equipment, and it's safe to do alone.

1. Pick something that makes you feel bad when you think about it. It could be a memory from the past, or a fear, such as spiders, heights, or speaking in public.

2. Sense how strong the feeling is. Is it a ten, the worst it could be, or a 0, and no bother to you at all?

3. With your hands on your thighs, pat your right and left leg back and forth at a comfortable rhythm.

4. While continuing to pat, recite an affirmation. This affirmation first states your uncomfortable feeling, then makes a strong positive statement. For example: "Even though I feel sad when I think about [my memory], I still love and accept myself, wholly and completely."

5. After a few minutes, stop and check in, going back to the original memory or fear. How strong is the feeling now? You will most likely find that it is much weaker.

The affirmation above is a sample that you may rewrite to suit your needs in the moment. The principle is to find a strong positive statement that will neutralize the negative feelings. Any positive statement that feels right for your situation will do; in my practice, I've found spiritual affirmations often prove to be very helpful.

You may also change the body tapping. Try folding your arms and tapping your biceps alternately, tapping your feet on the floor, or curling your toes in your shoes.

Turning 60 means that you don't have to carry the feelings and sensations of trauma with you anymore. Try WHEE, and as the negative emotions and thoughts leave you, you'll be ready to move on to the next adventure in your life!

4

"It's not too late to be what you might have been."

George Eliot

An alumna addresses a college reunion and finds the thread that links a diverse yet similar crowd.

by Alison Teal

For many years Alison Teal was a design and feature columnist for *The Denver Post*. A democratic political activist, she authored a blog, *Hot Flashes From The Campaign Trail*. She loves Brussels sprouts and is a very bad speller. She lives in Key West, Florida.

It's terrific to be here this weekend with all of you. How often do you get to have dinner in a room full of people every one of whom has this profoundly important common thread? We're all so different. We live in different places, we have different interests, different politics. Some are prosperous. Some have committed their lives to teaching, government, art, community service, or family. A few of you are gourmet cooks, while others eat nothing but roots and clouds. Some of you are famous, while others have preserved your precious anonymity. But with all of our differences we have this very fundamental thing in common. We are all remarkably old. I mean it; if you're sitting in this room tonight, you are probably pretty damn old.

I'm not sure when it happened, but I was shocked to wake up one morning and find that while I was asleep, I went completely out of style. It's like I went to bed as Gwyneth Paltrow and woke up as Bea Arthur. But it's not just the orthopedic shoes and Sheer Energy panty hose. It's parts of my body I didn't even know could go out of fashion. Have you been to a gym recently? How over the hill do you feel showering with all those Brazilian waxes? And then there's the amount of time we have to spend just to get out of the house . . . I'm not even talking about liposuction or Botox. I'm talking about fundamental things like hair — all that washing and blow-drying, cutting, coloring. And the hair on my head is the least of it. It is in fact the least of it. It's as if my hair follicles got bored over the years and now they've gotten together to try something new and more fun . . . like sprouting on my chin or a mole or just latching onto each other to form one really incredibly long eyebrow.

Remember Tolstoy talking about that sexy downy lip on Princess Lise? But of course, she was young. No one talks about my fetching downy lip. I'm sick of all the maintenance — the flossing, the moisturizing, the exercising, and — my God! — the dieting. I swear for 40 years there's been this thin person inside me screaming and screaming to get out. Fortunately through the years I've learned to give her cookies and alcohol and it shuts the bitch up.

The really frightening thing about middle age — and the fact is we all do think of ourselves as middle-aged, don't we? We've all bought right into the "60 is the new 40" thing, right? — well, then, the really frightening thing about middle age is that you know you'll grow out of it.

What's astonishing is that we even got to this advanced age. Think about it. It's amazing we even survived our childhoods. We didn't have seat belts or smoke alarms. We never wore crash helmets. We walked to school. Our milk was fortified mostly with Bosco, or, in a few cases, with some nice strontium-90. We engaged in all sorts of unsupervised activities — they called it "playing" back then. We developed immunity to childhood diseases the old-fashioned way — by catching them. Putting fluoride in the water was thought to be a communist plot — at least in Omaha, where we were ducking and covering under our protective wooden desks, which surprisingly were impervious to nuclear attack.

Our childhoods were difficult and exhausting in other ways, of course. Once television finally came to Omaha, I think we had only three channels and certainly no remote controls. You had to actually get up and walk over to the TV if you wanted to change the channel — which probably accounts for those endless hours of watching talking horses and flying nuns. And dancing cigarettes. Remember those? Commercials had a lot of dancing and singing in those days. Our parents were killing themselves with tobacco and alcohol, but they were really happy about it. And no one had ever even heard of secondhand smoke.

And the stuff we ate! We ate chocolate soldiers and cereal "shot from guns." We ate wax in the shape of big lips and that square bubble gum that came with baseball cards — not to mention those delicious candy cigarettes and bubble-gum cigars. And none of these treats had any limit on their shelf lives. We had actual sugar in our soft drinks. In the Midwest, mothers made sure we had something every day from what one of my brothers insists were the four primary food groups: pasta, potatoes, cakes, and pies. And here's a memory you've suppressed; our mothers actually cooked with lard. As in the phrase, commonly heard when I was a girl, "We're out of lard."

And yet . . . we all arrived at Smith College slim and fit — where many of us spent the first year in required calisthenic classes without ever even raising a sweat.

We've reminisced a lot this weekend about Smith in 1962 — it was a land of curfews, doors six inches open with three feet on the floor, special lates, and ironed sheets, along with big beef cheeseburger specials and Awful-Awfuls. Ah, but during our freshman year — and I swear, this is the truth — Diet Rite and Tab were introduced and Weight Watchers was founded. Our class has always been forward-looking. I believe we were the originators of the freshman 15.

It was so long ago we wrote papers on machines that are now in museums. We spoke to friends and parents on phones that were attached to a wall and when you were speaking to someone "long-distance," there was a hush of respect. Our tuition was $2,500 and we had six women of color in our class. We wore little red tunics. We were required to take Basic Motor Skills, which to my continuing astonishment had absolutely nothing to do with driving a car. Our stockings — when we weren't wearing kneesocks — were held up by girdles with legs in them. We also wore wraparound madras skirts, circle pins, wheat jeans, and penny loafers. . . . And if you were a really cool Easterner like my freshman roommate Sue Stanley, you wore them without socks.

We arrived at Smith with the Kennedy/Johnson administration in the midst of the Cuban Missile Crisis. Johnny Carson was taking over the *Tonight* show, Marilyn Monroe had just died of a drug overdose, and Jon Stewart had just been born. The Berlin Wall was a year old. John Glenn orbited the earth, Rachel Carson published *Silent Spring,* and Sylvia Plath committed suicide. And what were we doing? We were lining up like sheep having our posture pictures taken. What were we thinking?

But our time was at hand. We were avant-garde. We were in the forefront of the sexual revolution — which at the time was the world's third greatest revolution after the agrarian and the industrial. Now, we are at least surviving the fourth greatest revolution — the informational — and once again in the vanguard of the fifth: the cosmetic surgical.

And not only that, but for our whole lives we've been the muses for the pharmaceutical industry. We began right here with NoDoz. Then we paved the way with birth control pills followed shortly thereafter by fertility pills. We were the guinea pigs for diet pills, hormone replacement therapy, and now . . . of course . . . sleeping pills and antidepressants. If the drug companies made it, we ate it.

Over the last 40 years we've experienced upheaval and protests, escalating poverty, war — and that was just in our homes.
Like many of you, I didn't have a clue as to what I was going to do after Smith. Personally, I fit the profile in "Where the Girls Are," that lofty social guide to Eastern women's colleges written and published by the staff of the *Daily Princetonian.* When describing Smith they wrote, "The seniors . . . are easily recognizable as belonging to one of two categories: the smug, overly happy ones who are going to be married shortly after graduation; and the worried, nervous ones who haven't even been pinned."

This may have been right on target for a lot of us then, but let me tell you I googled each and every one of you — even accounting for your inflated resumes — and, come on, given that there are no records, who among us didn't get 1600 on our college boards? You are a staggeringly impressive group of women. To paraphrase another Smith alumna, Gloria Steinem, you became the men we wanted to marry.

But I'm not sure the evidence is in that we've made our times that much better. We ended our four years here during the time of an unpopular president involved in an immensely unpopular war.

Around the time of our commencement, Art Buchwald warned a graduating class: "We're leaving you a perfect world. Don't screw it up."

I'm not sure how to tell you all this. I mean you may not be aware of it yet. But the fact is, we did. We screwed it up. And I'm not even sure we can glue it back together. Personally, when I broke the part I was responsible for, I may have lost some of the pieces.

A lot was expected of us when we left Smith. We not only carried all the baggage of the past — obligations to family, friends, and society — but we felt an obligation to our newly emerging feminism. We were expected to be successful and productive as well as supportive and sexy; to forge new paths and break records and generally make it better for the women who would follow. That wasn't a bad thing but it didn't leave a lot of time — at least not for me — to figure out what I truly desired. Instead, I was overwhelmed by the expectations of others — sometimes burdened because those expectations were actually too minimal. Well, as George Eliot said, "It is never too late to be what you might have been."

The point is, we still have time. We weren't really the ones who broke that perfect world, but I believe we can help mend it. Okay, we've lost some of the pieces, but we're the kind of people who can make new ones — now, at this advanced age, more than ever. We've had our successes; we've conquered a lot of our fears. We know that things can go from better to bitter in an instant, but we also know they can go from bitter to better. We have mature hearts now. They've been broken and beaten and torn apart by life. And it's a good thing, because we can use that experience.

G. K. Chesterton said, ". . . the power of hoping through everything, the knowledge that the soul survives its adventures, that great inspiration comes to the middle-aged. God has kept that good wine until now."

Our parents actually left us a better world than they inherited — but then the world they inherited was a pretty crummy one. In some ways, we've had a harder job because we started with so much. What will future generations say about us? It's not too late to affect the answer to that question. This is the time in our lives when we can afford to ask "what if?" It's odd, but every defeat when you're young seems like the end of the world. With age comes patience and hope. Now is the time we can really make a difference. All of us, not just those of you who already have.

I'll end by telling you what I hope for us: that we will prove that Dorothy L. Sayers was right when she said, "Time and trouble will tame an advanced young woman, but an advanced old woman is uncontrollable by any earthly force."

5

Question everything

Revisit the rebellious spirit of your youth. Your 60s are a perfect time to revive the activism of the '60s!

by Leo Sewell

Leo Sewell is an internationally recognized found-object artist living in Philadelphia, Pennsylvania. His humorous, life-size sculptures of people and animal statues are in over 40 museums and in private collections worldwide. Ripley's owns 50 of his pieces, which are displayed in Ripley's Believe It Or Not! museums around the globe.

Now that I've turned 60, I realize that rebellion, independence, contrariness, and general opposition to authority are difficult to perpetuate in middle age. Yes, I consider 60 to be only middle age, although, even with the help of preservatives and vitamin supplements, I probably will not live to be 120.

As a child of the '60s and an admitted hippie, rebellion suited me well. I peed on the Pentagon, got gassed at the Justice Department, and experimented with my fair share of sex and drugs. God, Woodstock was a blast!

Many of my generation have, to varying degrees, consciously resisted being fit into a mold. We have choosen our clothes, hair, family, friends, and other modes of taste to express who we are, deep down inside. Yet, through the decades of life, degrees of conformity are meted out by many small, but continuous decisions. Many "squares" get ground down to fit into round holes.

A good question, it seems, is: "Why?"

As I look back and around, it seems to me that employers and family are the two great forces that mold conformity. It's the lucky few on the planet who manage to retain their individuality, and build successful careers expanding on their youthful rebellion. Jerry Garcia, Fidel Castro, Mick Jagger, and Allen Ginsberg are just a handful of these mavericks who come to mind.

I'm happy that I've managed to retain most of my hard edges, though far shy of the excesses of Jerry Garcia. For one thing, I haven't had a nine-to-five job since 1970, which is probably why I look forward to continuing my art "work" for at least the next 20 years.

Choosing to become an artist fit well with the '60s scene. It is, almost by definition, the ultimate "do your own thing." I took my rebellion further, in that I attended no art classes. My selection of found objects as my medium further placed me outside the mainstream.

I've enjoyed playing with other people's "junk" as far back as I can remember. It was 50 years ago that I discovered the Navy dump near my childhood home in Annapolis, Maryland. It seems like it was just yesterday. I can still clearly visualize the dump, overflowing with mechanical parts from planes and boats. I found great joy in taking the military's castaways apart and saving each piece. As my room became more cluttered, and the puritan ethos of our home more pronounced, it occurred to me to build or combine these pieces into something new. It wasn't really about art, at this point, but play — and the joy of the objects, and creation.

This passion basically went on until college, during which I was introduced to "serious" art. My rebellion was at its peak then, and I asked, "Why not continue to play and create with these found objects and call it art?" Marcel Duchamp (in my opinion, the greatest iconoclast and most important artist of the 20th century) became my hero and mentor. (I've heard it said that Andy Warhol explored one room in the mansion that Duchamp built. You'll get no argument from me.)

I took the time to get a graduate degree in art history, but in 1969, it was time to make my way in the world.

I remember thinking that I could try to maximize my income or try to minimize my needs. I embraced the latter, bought a $5,000 house, and did handyman jobs to have the time to refine my art. Still, it took decades of dedication to vision and technique to reach the level of success I enjoy around the globe today as a found-objects artist.

Perhaps it is that success, however, that has entwined me with the establishment I once eschewed. Rebellion or not, I have an insurance bill that must be paid on time, a vacation home, investments, and a wife and kid. My wife has been very accepting of my nonconformity, but my 19-year-old daughter is conformity itself. How did that happen?! I love my kid to death, but I think she should spend some time listening to George Carlin.

I don't profess to know all of life's answers. For a response to the big, mind-blowing question, "Why we are here?" I'll defer to Carlin. I will put this out there: I kinda think we're like ants on a rock. Some days, we're lucky we're not zapped by the sun through some brat's magnifying glass. Science, as explained by Karl Popper, is my god.

Since being contrary in "old" age is expected, maybe the rebellious thing for me to do is to be acceptant and nice. Let me sit with that a moment.

Moment over. Nah, not my style. At this point, though my rebellious streak has mellowed, I still want to be me.

Besides, it has been scientifically proven that ornery people live longer. I have a lot of years of living yet to do. My parting words of wisdom? Be a pain in the ass and do your own thing. Life is too damn short to be pushing paper if your soul aches to go skydiving. As for me, I'll be in my studio playing with my junk.

6

Go directly to jail

To all of the possessions, wealth. and acclaim you've accumulated in the past 60 years, add a little humility. There's nothing like spending some time in jail to teach you life's greatest lesson.

by Kathy J. Marshack, Ph.D., P.S.

Kathy Marshack, Ph.D., is a psychologist with more than 40 years experience as a marriage and family therapist, business coach and Asperger's Syndrome expert in Vancouver, Washington. (www.kmarshack.com) She is the author of four books including *Entrepreneurial Couples: Making It Work at Work and at Home.*

At the age of 54, I was arrested and put in jail. And though I wouldn't have believed it at the time, I learned a few valuable lessons I might never have otherwise.

In the holding tank, my cell mate was a beautiful young woman with long, dark, wavy hair and an angelic face, who was perspiring profusely and crying as she went through the throes of heroin withdrawal. Despite the situation, having a companion made us both feel better, and a little magic began to happen. As we sat and talked, I learned that she too had children and was worrying about them as I was about my own kids. We talked for a while, then sat quietly with our eyes shut, and I asked God to take care of both of us.

Soon, I needed to urinate, but the toilet seat was covered in other people's mess, and there was no toilet paper, anyway. Plus, the guards could watch everything, and they were all men. I just couldn't do it.

I searched for a distraction and remembered the phone on the wall. I thought I might try once more to reach my attorney or my children. I had already been stripped of my clothing, even my bra, since it had underwire (apparently, a potential prison weapon). I was dressed in the typical, navy-blue jail clothes and plastic sandals. No pockets, no belt, no bra. I wondered how I would make a call without my calling card or a credit card. The instructions on the wall were specific, though: either you paid in advance, or called "collect." They'd already taken my purse, so "collect" was my only option. Since my luck was running poorly that day and the phone was always busy, I could not get a call out of the place.

I was starting to feel desperate, and told myself I had to get a grip on reality. I was not going anywhere soon!

My companion was booked long before I was, and by the time my turn came, I was curious about the procedure. The sergeant in charge questioned me briefly. Then my picture was taken with a funny little camera in the ceiling. I had to roll my eyes almost to the back of my head for the shot, and later, when I saw my picture, I realized that it made me look like a serial killer! It's not a look that works very well in jail.

Next was fingerprinting. I'd expected an ink pad and pen, but this jail was modern. Computers take pictures of your fingerprints, and the data, I assume, is whisked away via the Internet to the FBI and the CIA.

Then, the sergeant made a list of my belongings. Thank God, I had cash, because credit cards don't work in jail. With cash, I could buy a toothbrush, toothpaste, a comb, and a cup. If you can't buy a cup, you don't have anything from which to drink. I felt privileged to have a cup.

At the time of my arrest, I was in the middle of a divorce from my husband, a local divorce attorney. Once I filed the paperwork for the split, I expected he would fight me tooth and nail. As the situation dragged on into year two, my patience wore thin. One day, I just broke down under the pressure of mounting legal fees, caring for two teenage children (one of whom is autistic), managing a full caseload as a psychologist in private practice, and a recent diagnosis of cancer. Before I knew what was happening, I was cast as the lead in a melodramatic domestic-violence scene. And poof! I was arrested for giving my ex-husband's secretary a black eye.

The experience was a turning point in my life. I had lessons to learn that heretofore had been ignored, and now there was no getting around it. The truth is, I probably wouldn't have listened any other way; I needed to be humbled, I needed to learn to stop using just my mind and learn to open my heart instead. So, on that first night of jail, I let go of fear.

I suppose that among the "60 things to do when you turn 60," going to jail is not really one of them. But the lessons I learned from this experience, hard as they were, should be high on everyone's list. All of your education, possessions, and accomplishments are an illusion. It's not that you aren't supposed to enjoy the benefits of living on planet Earth. It's just that God created this material world for us so that we could grow spiritually, not just climb the corporate ladder. Earth can be harsh and cruel. But your spirit is a loving, beautiful thing; let it shine through in all that you do. Then divorce, health problems, financial woes, and all the other crises we face won't seem so hard to bear.

Once you get this lesson, you are ready to be The Teacher. Our country needs older, wiser, compassionate warriors to lead the younger ones to a more enlightened way of being. I think that is what turning 60 means . . . to become The Teacher.

Do unto others

All roads merge at 60! Keep your eye on the path ahead — it's time to channel the idealism of your youth into the very real need to give back to your community.

by Gerald S. Migdol

Gerald S. Migdol, Esq., is the founder and president of The Migdol Organization, which has owned, developed, and managed low- and middle-income housing, primarily in Harlem and the Bronx, since 1975. The company specializes in the renovation of multifamily properties and the rehabilitation and conversion of brownstones into middle-income condominiums.

Many years ago, I heard an aphorism that supposedly came from Winston Churchill: "Those who aren't idealists at 20 and realists at 40 haven't fully lived." As I approach the venerable age of 60, I realize that a mingling of the two provides the healthiest outlook and the most effective results.

I was born in 1950 to working-class parents and raised to be educated, respectful, hardworking, skillful, and self reliant. When I was in my 20s, the Vietnam War and the Civil Rights Movement were at the forefront of American life, and they had a profound and lasting impact on my development. I could not ignore obvious social injustices, nor could I support a war with dubious objectives, which was why I was attracted to the idealistic Hippie Movement. I loved the camaraderie and solidarity that I found with new and diverse people unified by a desire for peace, harmony, and societal change. I took part in radical protests and campus takeovers, and eventually dropped out of college — disillusioned with the contemporary values that seemed driven by self-interest and a lack of concern for others. I refused to fully engage in an establishment that I viewed as unfair and unjust, so I followed a path more aligned with my changing mores. I was a rebel with a cause.

In the ensuing years, I strove to perfect romantic visions of communal reform, all the while perfecting my skills in the field of building construction. Throughout my 20s, I worked enthusiastically as a carpenter, plumber, and electrician, helping to build homes and businesses for people within our movement. Before I hit 30, I met and married the woman of my dreams — Sheri Perl — a wonderfully caring person filled with beauty, inside and out, and imbued with similar idealistic visions of transformation.

Sheri's childhood struggles with Crohn's disease (which ultimately led her down a path to help others in need) ruled out natural childbirth. Thus, over the next decade, we adopted three wonderful children. To increase my earning capacity, I reentered college and went on to law school, simultaneously forging a business in real estate and construction. The practical demands of rearing a family and growing a business put my romantic visions of reform on hold. By my late 30s, I had achieved a fair amount of financial success in real estate. With that success came a heightened sense of realism and pragmatism. Still, I always kept my younger ideals close to my heart.

In the early 1990s, while I was in my 40s, real estate — and my business — took a nosedive. I lost most of my buildings, closed my offices, and took employment as a developer of properties for others, including banks and large institutions. Over the next ten years, I rebuilt more than 3,000 inner-city apartments in countless housing complexes throughout many of the larger East Coast cities, including New York, Newark, Philadelphia, Hartford, Ft. Lauderdale, and Miami.

In the late 1990s, after surviving two bankruptcy filings, I again started to rebuild my business by purchasing and developing vacant properties in Harlem, New York. And it was there, in Harlem, that all the roads I had traveled converged, and I found my true calling.

I am still actively contributing to the revival of this great historical and cultural area — developing brownstones and multifamily housing for low- and middle-income families. I promoted home ownership for first-time buyers and created affordable condos for civil-servant workers. I built my offices and a family residence within the community, hired my workers from the area, and achieved financial success. These efforts opened new doors for my family to give back to a community that needed help in so many ways. In 2004, we established the Migdol Family Foundation, which assists individuals and families with health care, education, employment, housing, and general welfare. Through this philanthropy and community outreach, my life has become richer and more satisfying. I know this work will be the centerpiece of my remaining years. I now realize that what moves me is not only the donation of money, but the giving of time and energy to the people and causes in which I believe.

This is something that almost everyone who approaches 60 can do. Our children are older now and no longer demand as much time or focus. We are freer now to explore new goals and opportunities in the world of philanthropic giving. I feel confident that this caring and sharing will bring new levels of self-realization and fulfillment.

It has been said that good leaders are pragmatic and realistic in design and approach, yet still keep their visions within sight and talk the language of the idealist. As I near 60, I now understand that life is not about extremes; it's not that idealism or realism should win out, but rather there should be a blend of the two. It is not about revolutionary societal change, but incremental help from everyone — one dollar and one person at a time.

Sixty years represents a lot of living, which has given me a clearer vision of the path that lies ahead. I realize that all of our experiences, good and bad, equal the sum total of who we have become. The many roads we've traveled have brought us to where we are today. All eyes point forward; there is no turning back. So relax, focus clearly on the road ahead, and enjoy your life — by giving and doing for others. It is truly the road to happiness.

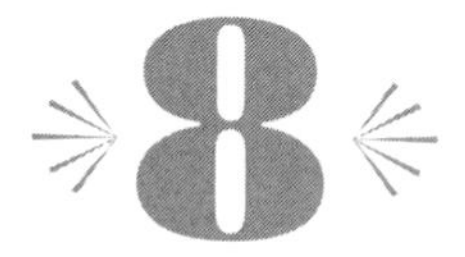

Follow your passions

At this stage of life, let your passions be your legacy. Endow the futures of others.

by Seawell J. Brandau

Seawell J. Brandau sold a third-generation printing business at the age of 65, when he was "young enough to have a second career." A former president of Label Printing Industries of America, he was also president of Senior Citizens, Inc., in Nashville, Tennessee, before he was a senior citizen. Mr. Brandau was the developer of the mentoring program Personal Growth Strategies, served as administrator of the Leave A Legacy program for the Community Foundation of Middle Tennessee, and edited the "Gifts and Talents for Lay Ministry" workshops.

If what you're looking for is the right time to plan for a rich and fulfilling next phase of life, then 60 is a fine age! You don't have to sell the family business, as I did, to enter this "enrichment era" of life. Just take the time to consider how passion, together with thoughtful reflection, can lead to new opportunities.

For me, as a third-generation business owner, I was

faced with the typical conditions at our regional family printing company: the increasing squeeze from larger, national companies with greater capital bases, and unfortunately, no executive successor in sight. I knew that selling the business was the right decision, but I had no definite plans. Instead, my personal desire was to be young enough to explore new careers. How to proceed?

After selling the business, a time of "grief" followed; this was the transition period from the day-to-day work schedules, goals, and plans I was familiar with into "none of the above." That first weekday morning with nowhere to go was a shock. And the phrase "no pay-check, no value" seemed very real to me. This wouldn't have been as hard if I'd seen it for what it was — a period of change. What was required was to step back, listen to my inner self, and talk to others who had been in the same situation. Patience and passion were the qualities I needed most at this stage of my future planning.

I looked deep inside myself. What was I passionate about? What did I dwell on? What excited me? Was it individual achievement? Adventure? Making the world a better place? Deeper spiritual involvement? Quiet, thoughtful enhancement of my mind? Creative writing? Health enhancement? Golf? Fishing?

I tried another exercise: throughout my life, I have

wondered, "What small accomplishments have made me proud?" I wrote these accomplishments down, and also jotted down exactly why I was proud of each one. I then pondered my list, looking for any clues or patterns about my passions. As I dwelled on these areas, I felt bursts of energy and the desire to do more.

Before jumping into any major project, I got involved in small ventures, to test possibilities. Then, I evaluated whether I would want to invest time, money, or energy in each one. If my answer was yes to the investment of time and energy, then I realized passion was there. Passion helps you focus your vision and propels you in a certain direction; it can also sustain you over the rough spots. It adds energy and optimism. One of the benefits of being at my (our) stage in life is that we have the time to try an assortment of activities — without having to make long-term commitments.

One of these projects evolved into a mentoring program, Personal Growth Strategies. In it, we worked with the positive aspects of a client's life and built on that person's "good news" first. Then, after laying the groundwork, we looked at weaknesses, or what was holding someone back. Using aspects of a client's own success as a base, we suggested positive steps to deal with the weaknesses. Listening, reflection, and feedback all became part of the lineup in the growth process.

Passion also led me to the realization that we are all the beneficiaries of the legacies of our predecessors. I wanted to ensure that the ability to leave a legacy became an opportunity that could be shared by everyone who desired to do so. As a result, I have become more passionate and practical in encouraging the spirit of generosity. I have become dedicated to educating and encouraging people to add to the endowments of churches and other charities through the program Leave a Legacy, a project from the Community Foundation of Middle Tennessee. Endowment gifts live forever; they provide resources for proclaiming the faith, caring for the needy, educating youth, appreciating the arts, sustaining the environment, and other "passionate causes," a gift that has the potential to live beyond your grandchildren's grandchildren.

From the fulfilling events of our past, from our passions, and from our wishes for future generations come many clues for the giving-back portion of our lives today. It's exciting to rise each morning — filled with drive, energy, and positive opportunities to make a difference in our own lives, as well as the lives of others. It is possible to create your own legacy.

Make a difference

Put your energy and drive behind a cause you're passionate about. It's never too late to make your mark!

by Suzanne Wright

Suzanne Wright was the cofounder (with her husband, Bob Wright, chairman and CEO of NBC Universal) of Autism Speaks (www.autismspeaks.org), a nonprofit organization devoted to finding a cure for autism. She was on the board of directors of the Make-A-Wish Foundation of Metro New York, the Laura Pels Foundation, the Inner-City Foundation for Charity and Education, and the Philadelphia-based Champions of Caring Project. Ms. Wright passed away in 2016.

Entering my seventh decade, I feel that my life is full in the deepest sense. I have a wonderful family, work that challenges and inspires me, and personal accomplishments of which I'm proud. Far from feeling as if things are starting to slow down, I'm filled with the sense they are just getting started. For starters, I only recently finished college, and a year ago founded, with my husband, a national nonprofit organization to help find a cure for autism. I hope my experiences prove inspirational for all those entering their golden years. Keep forging ahead, making plans, and meeting new challenges. I've learned that it's never too late to pursue your dreams; you're never too old to take on new challenges. Indeed, as I look ahead, I'm hopeful that the best is yet to come.

Keep your dream alive

I had always wanted to go to college, but sometimes life has other plans. In my case, I married my high school sweetheart soon after I graduated. Bob was in law school when we married; I worked to help support us. Soon afterward, we started having children. As a young stay-at-home mother and supportive wife, I set aside my own dream of a college education.

By the time I was in my 40s and my children were heading off to college, my husband had become a high-profile executive in the entertainment industry. I had taken on a more prominent role as well, with a good deal of charity work filling my calendar and giving me a great sense of satisfaction. Still, I felt something was missing. My dream of going to college had never really died. As my children left home to pursue their dreams, I decided to do the same.

It wasn't easy entering college as a grown woman. Frankly, I was terrified. I enrolled at Sarah Lawrence College, taking continuing-education classes and ultimately matriculating as an undergraduate. I'm proud that in 1998 I graduated with a Bachelor of Arts degree.

My family's biggest challenge came in March 2004, the day we heard the heartbreaking news that our first grandson, Christian, had autism. At the time of his diagnosis, I knew very little about the disorder. But I quickly immersed myself in learning everything possible, because I so desperately wanted to help Christian and support my daughter and son-in-law, who were overwhelmed and suffering.

I learned that no one seemed to have any answers. The cause of autism remains a mystery; there is no known cure, and experts disagree on the best treatments. There are many options, yet little guidance from the medical community. When my daughter first raised concerns to her doctor about Christian's changing behavior — the first sign that something might be wrong — he told her not to worry, that boys develop more slowly than girls. Had we known the early signs of autism, we might have gotten him diagnosed and treated earlier, giving him a better chance at recovery. In the end — like every family struggling with this diagnosis — we settled on what we felt was the best treatment plan, with the little guidance we received.

Part of the problem is that autism research remains severely underfunded, compared to other childhood diseases. The nation's fastest-growing serious developmental disorder, autism today affects one in 166 children — up from one in 10,000 children a dozen years ago. Yet it's amazing that this growing epidemic — a new case is diagnosed almost every 20 minutes — has yet to receive substantial awareness or funding. It's time to change that.

I decided I'd have to do something myself. I experienced how emotionally and physically exhausting it is to care for an autistic child, and how financially and emotionally devastating it can be for so many families. There is an 80 percent divorce rate for couples with an autistic child. I realized that by bringing this health crisis to the national stage, my husband, Bob, and I could bring something new to the table.

We launched Autism Speaks (www.autismspeaks.org) a year after Christian was diagnosed. Our mission is to promote awareness about autism and to raise money to quicken the pace of biomedical research. It has been a tremendous undertaking, and I'm amazed at what we have accomplished so quickly. Much work remains to be done, but we have a great team of people working with us, who are just as committed and passionate as we are. We're building on the hard work and energy of the many committed parents and activists who've been involved with this issue for a long time.

Founding Autism Speaks has been healing for me, and also cathartic — it helped me channel my tremendous grief into something productive and which I hope will make a difference in the life of every person affected by autism. The autism community is incredibly passionate and committed. But until now, it hasn't had a strong, unified voice on the national level. Through Autism Speaks, I'm convinced we'll dramatically change the field of autism research and treatment and begin finding the answers that families so desperately need.

The truth is, anyone can make a difference in the issues or areas he or she cares about. Bob and I are obviously not first to take on the challenge of autism. I am endlessly inspired by the many wonderful people who have started autism advocacy organizations from their kitchen tables and grown them into large, effective groups, while also dealing with the demands of an autistic child. These activists have paved the way for Autism Speaks. And they remind us that—with enough determination, passion, and courage—anyone can make a difference. That's as true in your 60s as it was in your 20s. It's up to you to let your passions create the life you want to lead.

Section Two

I'M A BELIEVER

(The Monkees, 1966)

10

Find your island

When it comes to creative endeavors, the best path for this acclaimed artist has been solitude.

by Jamie Wyeth

James Browning Wyeth was born on July 6, 1946, in Wilmington, Delaware, just south of Chadds Ford, Pennsylvania, where he grew up. Since adolescence he has attracted considerable attention as a third-generation American artist: the son of Andrew Wyeth, among the country's most popular painters, and the grandson of Newell Convers Wyeth, famous for his distinctive illustrations for the classic novels of Stevenson, Cooper, and Scott. "Everybody in my family paints — excluding possibly the dogs," says Jamie Wyeth. He now divides his time between Chadds Ford and Southern Island, Maine.

You've probably heard the expression "No man is an island." I rigorously disagree. Indeed, I think people are individual, unique "islands" — and they need to carefully guard their shorelines against the distractions and intrusions of the world.

That's one reason I have spent much of my life in Maine.

For many years I lived on the island of Monhegan. It's a lovely, isolated place. But even its community of 60 people got to be too much for me. So I bought a private, 22-acre island in the early 1990s. There's only one structure — a lighthouse (I use the attached keeper's cottage as my house) — and just one person: me.

I physically spend eight to nine months there. I do nothing but take walks, stare at the sea, and paint. My daily ritual rarely varies: I work pretty much all day every day. Does that make me sound boring? Maybe. But the environment offers just what I need. It's the only place, in fact, where I can fully concentrate on my painting. It's my oasis of focus, if you will.

Of course, not everyone wants to live on an island. Many people wouldn't appreciate the isolation. But I don't need a lot of human interaction — nor am I required to sit in a cubicle all day or attend board meetings. So it suits me perfectly. I find painting is something I do better alone.

And I would argue that painting is as difficult as brain surgery. It requires great discipline. Perhaps that discipline makes it easier for me to shut out much of the world around me. When my grandfather and father were growing up, there were much fewer stimuli; they didn't have to self-impose as much as I do. They were able to find the right atmospheres they needed to paint. But today it's a different world.

Now, we're daily, hourly, bombarded with too much information. Take the mail. Thirty years ago people waited in anticipation for the mail drop. Now, we dread it. Sure, I get the same bills and junk mail that you do, but their unwanted appearance moves me to eliminate and simplify. Now that I'm 60, I feel even more strongly the need to slash and chop. "Weed Out" has become my mantra.

Yet there's an upside to my overwhelming drive for simplification. It's given me something many people lack: focus. The whole notion of my living on an island isn't an accident. It's to focus my head and my eyes. To find the simple satisfaction of being alone, and to pare down in my paintings until I reach the simplicity I'm after.

But I've discovered this truth: to be alone is not to be lonely. That's very much a misconception. Even I am not a complete hermit. I have a wife, to whom I've been married to for 30 years. But we're not together constantly, and we believe our times apart bring a new dynamic to our relationship. Like me, she covets the space to do her own work.

Am I saying you should physically remove yourself from your relationships? Even move to an island? No. But you must carve out time to be alone. You can have a dynamic marriage and family life and still find your island. It just takes focus.

Here's what I mean. I live in New York City part of the year. During those visits, I want to see every film, every play, just like other visitors. But my brief stays remind me anew of the danger in seeking to be entertained every minute. I have to leave or I'll never get any work done.

Yet it is in Manhattan, surrounded by the millions who inhabit that very large island, that I remind myself that I can create a mental island. You can do it too, by adding blinders. Just choose to reduce the amount of stuff you let in.

And stop watching so much television! When I paint children, people often suggest that I use TV to get the kids to sit quietly. But as a device for painting it just doesn't work. What it does do is put them into an unthinking state. It is mindless entertainment that turns them into little robots. Who wants to paint that?

If the thought of isolating yourself stresses you out, I suggest you look at it differently. It is only when you are willing to go there, to eliminate all outside distractions, that you discover your true self and your unique talents.

Being alone — and being satisfied in that solitude — is incredibly fulfilling. It's also productive, if my number of paintings is any indication.

Obviously, I'm trying to talk you into paring down. Or maybe I'm just trying to explain why I think it's helpful, especially in our 60s. In fact, I view turning 60 as a yardstick, a way of defining my way of life for the next 10 years. What I hope comes out of this conscious choice is a more effective life, and better work. So shut out, peel away, and focus. Find the quiet so your inner voice can be heard loud and clear. Then do what it says. That's where you'll find your island.

11

Dare to believe in ghosts

Now that you're closer to heaven than birth, open your mind to the possibility of intangibles. Believe in the mystery of life — and beyond!

by Mark Nesbitt

Mark Nesbitt was a National Park Service ranger/historian for five years at Gettysburg before starting his own research and writing company. Since then he has published 14 books, including the award-winning *Ghosts of Gettysburg* series. Mr. Nesbitt's stories have been seen on the History Channel, A&E, the Discovery Channel, the Travel Channel, *Unsolved Mysteries*, and numerous regional television shows, and have been heard on *Coast to Coast AM* and regional radio. In 1994, he created the commercially successful *Ghosts of Gettysburg Candlelight Walking Tours* and in 2006, the *Ghosts of Fredericksburg Tours.*

"The best and most beautiful things in the world cannot be seen or even touched. They must be felt within the heart." — *Helen Keller*

Major General Joshua L. Chamberlain, a key participant in the Battle of Gettysburg, July 1–3, 1863, was asked as an old man whether the rumor was true that the ghost of George Washington was seen that first dark night of the watershed Civil War battle, on a white horse, leading his column of marching men toward the blood-soaked battlefield. Who knows what Chamberlain might have said as a prewar, mid-30s, staid college professor, ruminating in the mellow pedantry of his classroom? He was, however, asked after he had seen young men torn apart in battle by cannon shot, or liquefied as they charged against canister shells, or as they lay quietly dying, their souls transmigrating before his very eyes. He, himself, had had a glimpse into the next world after being shot during a charge at Petersburg, Virginia.

"Yes," he replied to the question about Washington, dead 64 years before being seen riding toward Gettysburg. "I heard the rumor come down the column. Doubtless it was a superstition." Then he paused, for quite a while, as if remembering all he had seen and been through, and continued, "But who among us can say that such a thing is impossible?"

Thus was born the very first ghost story about the Battle of Gettysburg.

Since Major General Chamberlain's admission, thousands of anecdotal stories of bizarre, personal, paranormal experiences on the great battlefield in Pennsylvania have been related. After I wrote the first (of six) *Ghosts of Gettysburg* book, I received letters, faxes, photos, and phone calls from normal, sane, everyday people who had experienced an unexplainable, paranormal event while visiting Gettysburg. Their experiences range from the sounds of volleys of musketry, 140-odd years after they were fired, to ancient military airs wafting from long-abandoned woods, to sightings of entire regiments maneuvering in 19th century tactical formations before astounded crowds, then suddenly vanishing. I have personally collected well over 700 stories — and those are just the ones people decide to share. There have been hundreds more from other allegedly haunted sites around the country. There really does seem to be something going on all around us, sometimes seen and sometimes not, wherever we happen to be, unexplainable by logic or science.

But it is not new. Neanderthals, 70,000 years ago, buried their dead with food, weapons, and clothing for the afterlife. Egyptians mummified the bodies of their dead so that they might appear and be recognized in the Great Beyond. Shakespeare's best plays involved ghosts; young Hamlet was driven, some claim, to insanity, by his father's ghost beseeching revenge. Ghosts have been smelled, felt, heard (61 percent of all my stories are auditory apparitions), and seen (only 11 percent are visual), which moves it all from the realm of "do you believe in ghosts?" to "do you believe in the human senses?"

If you believe in the human sense of hearing or sight, and the utter astonishment of the witnesses who have heard and seen these amazing things, then you must believe in ghosts.

Still, there are the doubters along with the believers.

Those who don't believe in ghosts have good company. No less a personage than Aristotle was absolutely certain there were no ghosts. Yet, centuries later, the great French mathematician and philosopher René Descartes was just as certain that there must be. Most of us nonphilosopher types, when we were children, were sure there were ghosts. (I know I was afraid of them.) Still, our own government, through the National Park Service at Gettysburg, denies the existence of spirits on the battlefield.

Many believe that ghosts should be relegated to children's pastimes, or tales told around a campfire or whispered at a slumber party.

As we approach three score, it just might be a good idea to start believing in ghosts again. And it is not just because, at 60, we are closer to being one than ever before. There are plenty of other reasons to believe in ghosts.

After all these years, we should have realized that we cannot ignore something, whistling while passing graveyards, just because we want to. Like Major General Chamberlain, we have all seen enough to realize there are things in this world, such as cruelty, war, and mindless, incomprehensible hate, that we do not, and perhaps cannot ever, understand.

We should believe in ghosts because they represent something simple — our youth, and a remarkably good tale told by the best storyteller in the crowd. We should also believe in them, though, because they represent something complicated — our impending, inexorable old age and the other story of life — which is death.

Believe in ghosts so that you then can believe in things that you cannot see, hear, smell, or prove to exist, but that have been floating, ghostlike, around us for six decades: things like love, honor, fealty, romance, faith, hope, and all those other precious, ephemeral things in our lives that are intangible, but undeniable.

Believe in ghosts because their existence signifies what the prophets have promised humankind: that we will meet again those we love and cherish here on earth, and meet them as we were meant to be — pure, unadulterated, burnished souls, purified by death and cleansed of this temptation-filled world. It certainly removes the sting of death to believe that we shall again be with all those once-living beings we have ever loved, and who have ever loved us. And this is why it is important that there have been reports of animal ghosts: What an afterlife it will be if we can be with our beloved animal companions, again! I don't know about you, but there, for me, will be heaven.

Believe in ghosts so that you can believe in the hereafter — that death is not a closing door, but one that is opening.

Believe in ghosts so that you can believe there is something more than mere life.

Believe in ghosts because it just may be that the only purpose of this great mystery we call life is to teach us about that other, greater mystery — death.

"In great deeds something abides. On great fields something stays. Forms change and pass; bodies disappear; but spirits linger, to consecrate ground for the vision-place of souls."

— Major General Joshua L. Chamberlain, age 60,
October, 1889, speaking at Gettysburg

12

Be a saint

Being holy simply means being who you are.
Embrace your true self!

by Father James Martin, S.J.

Father James Martin, S.J., a graduate of the Wharton School of Business, spent six years in the corporate world before entering the Jesuits. During his Jesuit training, he spent two years working with refugees in East Africa, helping them to start their own small businesses. Father Martin is editor-at-large of *America*, a Catholic magazine, and author of several books, including *Becoming Who You Are* and his memoir, *My Life with the Saints.*

For many people — even for the wisest 60-year-old — holiness seems pretty boring.

In popular culture and the contemporary imagination, holy men and women are often depicted as leading dull lives — splitting their time between praying for hours and walking around with (literally) holier-than-thou expressions on their sour faces. If they ever get off their knees, it is only to take time to dole out some gruel to the poor.

Hardly the sort of people you'd want to spend a weekend with. "I'd rather laugh with the sinners than cry with the saints," sang Billy Joel, a few decades ago.

Even a quick glance at the stories of the saints — from every faith tradition — shows otherwise. They led lives that were the opposite of dull, and they were nothing if not human.

Take Saint Francis of Assisi. To many people, Francis is nothing more than a good-natured hippie who liked animals and prayed for peace. He's a nonthreatening guy. That's why people feel comfortable placing his statue in their backyard garden. But the real Francis, who lived in the 13th century, was far more lively and hotheaded than his garden-variety stereotype.

Here was a person, after all, who proved that he was no longer under the command of his father, a wealthy cloth merchant of Assisi, by stripping naked in the town square and depositing his clothes at his father's feet. Later in life, when he stumbled upon a tiny house that his followers had built for themselves, Francis was so enraged by what he saw as their refusal to live simply that he climbed atop the roof and began tearing the house apart. No one in Assisi would have described Francis as boring.

"Crazy" would have been the more popular adjective.

Holiness doesn't mean that you are averse to the occasional joke or prank. It's unlikely that the saints would have attracted so many admirers had they not had a well-developed sense of humor. Nor would they have been able to appreciate life as much as they obviously did. As the saying goes, the surest sign of God's presence is joy. In the late 1950s, a journalist asked the jovial Pope John XXIII how many people worked in the Vatican. After a pause, the Pope laughed and said, "About half of them!"

Nor were even the holiest of men and women immune to some doubt — often long-lasting. Perhaps this is where their lives intersect most closely with our own. After the death of Mother Teresa, described in her own lifetime as a "living saint," her secret papers revealed that she had struggled with an intense spiritual darkness for many years.

In a letter to a friend, she wrote candidly that she faced terrible feelings of "God not wanting me, of God not being God, and of God not really existing." It was a shocking revelation to some of Mother Teresa's admirers, but maybe it shouldn't have been: she was human, after all.

In time, the "Saint of the Gutters" came to accept these feelings as a way to identify with the abandonment felt by the poor with whom she worked, and with the rejection that Jesus of Nazareth experienced during his Passion. Overall, the life of the woman now known as Blessed Teresa of Calcutta shows that even the saints struggled with their spiritual lives — often more than the rest of us.

This isn't just the case with Christianity. The Hebrew Scriptures show that Moses doubted his ability to carry out what God asked him to do. When he stands before the burning bush (a fairly convincing spectacle, if you ask me), Moses asks God how he can ever lead the Hebrew people out of Egypt.

Moses, it seems, had a speech impediment. "I am slow of speech and slow of tongue," he says in a touching admission of his humanity. And so one of the holiest of people in the Judeo-Christian tradition was given to some doubt.

What each of these men and women had in common was that they eventually embraced their individual humanity. They realized that all God was calling them to be was who they were. God had called Moses with his stutter, Mother Teresa with her doubt, and Francis of Assisi with his short temper. God was asking them to be themselves.

That's a powerful message — especially in a world that tells you that you need to be someone else to be happy, or be different to be fulfilled. Too often we say to ourselves, "If only I were this or that person, then my life would be better."

As an older Jesuit once told me: "Compare and despair!" In other words, if you keep comparing yourself to someone else, you may never fully appreciate the person whom God has created. Sure, we're meant to emulate other holy people from our religious traditions — but we're not meant to be them. We're meant to be uniquely ourselves. That's something of what the psalmist meant when he wrote in Psalm 139, "For I am fearfully and wonderfully made."

Sixty is a fine time to finally set aside the false comparisons that keep us from accepting who we are, and from embracing our true selves. The person God really wants us to be is pretty wonderful. It's time to see that the bumper sticker is right: "God doesn't make crap!"

In the late 1940s, the Trappist monk Thomas Merton wrote, "For me to be a saint means to be myself." As 60 approaches, when many people deepen their desire for a more spiritual life, they might turn to the examples of the saints who have gone before us — in every religious tradition. They teach us that being holy may not mean changing, it may simply mean being more of who you already are.

13

Set your intention

The mystical meaning of the number six shows potential balance and harmony in your 60s. Make that potential real by finding an intention to guide you in this decade.

by Catherine Shainberg, Ph.D.

Catherine Shainberg, Ph.D., grew up in England and France. She trained as an art historian at the School of the Louvre, earned a Masters from the Sorbonne, and was a consultant for Unesco. In 1972, she moved to Israel, where she converted to Judaism and spent ten years studying the Kabbalah of Light in Jerusalem with Madame Colette Aboulker-Muscat, a recognized Kabbalist, mystic, and teacher. She is the founder of the School of Images® and has over 40 years' experience in adapting traditional practices into a modern medical context. She is author of *Kabbalah and the Power of Dreaming: Awakening the Visionary Self* and *Genesis and Movement*. Catherine lives in New York City. She conducts imagery and dreaming workshops internationally.

The Kabbalists say that at 40 we are responsible for our face. What happens when we turn 50 or 60? We are not told, but numbers give us a clue. Numbers in Kabbalah, as in the dream world, are a language of condensed meaning.

Take four and five. Four is the number of manifestation. We need four corners to solidly establish the foundations of a house, a chair, a table. Five is a number of movement out into the world. We have five senses to perceive reality and twice five fingers, twice five toes to act in the world. What about six? What happens to us when we are six or 60? When we are 46, and six modifies the four? Six brings in the possibility of harmonious balance.

How do we know this? Because we have been given the Star of David. The star, which is two interlocked triangles, is balanced. One triangle points downward, the other points upward, so that together they form a six-pointed star with a hexagonal center.

The downward pointing triangle is traditionally seen as male, the upward pointing triangle as female. When the descent into and the rising toward harmonize, a happy union occurs, a relationship of peers. Six is the number of a happy marriage. If you are right now in a relationship, and are turning 60, expect the small irritations and difficulties in your togetherness to smooth out. You are scheduled for a rebirth of love and joyous harmony together.

The two triangles together, with their abstract representation of two arms, two legs, a head, and a sex, is the androgynous Adam, the man/woman first being of Genesis, to whose perfection you can aspire to return.

It illustrates the harmonious balance of our male and female characteristics, of our left and right brains, of our mind and our body. In kabbalistic terms it is the balance of the six lower sephirot or wheels of energy on the Tree of Life. When we are in perfect dynamic balance there is nothing to fear, and our heart can open up, which is called Tipheret or Beauty. When six comes into our numbers, whether in our age or in our dreams, then the possibility of having a peaceful and compassionate heart is at hand.

At six or at 60, we are in a biological possibility of balance. At six we have only one year of playful delight and harmony, but at 60 we have ten years, a whole cycle! Think of what you can do with that.

Do not think of the triangles of the star of David as fixed but as constantly moving to meet and interact with each other. The star hides a secret, one that is best understood with breathing. Let's imagine that the triangle going up is your breathing out, and the triangle going down is your breathing in. The movements of these two triangles are in response to each other, first one, then the other, respond in a rhythmic manner. If you breathe out, the breathing in will happen on its own, without effort. You can surrender to breathing out, because by emptying yourself, you will be filled — you call down what the kabbalists call Shefa, the Divine Influx from above.

That feeling is what your 60s can bring you, but remember, for the moment we are talking potential only. You must make it happen.

Let us assume that in your 40s you established yourself firmly in your career, while in your 50s you were very competitive and driven to accomplish all your goals. Now in your 60s, you can relax and bask in all that you have accomplished. No more need to compete, your children are settled in their own lives, and you can look forward to . . . retirement? Yes and no. You are not retiring from life! Finally you can think of yourself, enjoy who you are, cultivate your garden, be at peace. Finally you can breathe out and expect — "know" in the Biblical sense of experiencing fully — that you will be filled.

What if your unfolding hasn't happened as planned? Nothing is lost. Numbers are the language of the subconscious, of your dreaming. Return to your dreaming. In the dreaming, there is no linear time. You can accomplish what still needs to be accomplished in an instant: visualize what you need to enhance your 60s.

Breathe out slowly three times.

Go back to early childhood and recognize your life dreams. Then go forward in time, seeing what fears have blocked you from fully accomplishing your life dreams.

Now imagine that miraculously you are six years old today.

Retrace your path through your life, facing your fears and finding a playful way to conquer them. Bring your feeling of accomplishment and success through your new past right up to the new present.

Now see yourself in six weeks' time, free of fear. What are you doing? And in six months' time? In six years' time? Know that you have set yourself a kavanah, an intention. Trust in your intention by writing it down in gold letters in the center of a six-pointed star.

Open your eyes, seeing your six-pointed star with open eyes, and your intention in gold lettering at its center. Know that you have set your intention in motion.

Dreaming is very powerful. Our dreaming sets our actions in motion. By returning to your dreaming, you correct the past and project your present into your future by placing your kavanah into your own star. Through your breathing, you empty yourself, and then you are in perfect balance to receive. For the promise is that by breathing out, you will be filled. Expect balance and harmony. Love will come to you, peace will be with you. They are the promise of your 60s; enjoy it.

14

Pray

Prayer can be an ongoing conversation and constant companion, no matter what lies ahead.

by Leslie Williams, Ph.D.

Leslie Williams is the author of *When Women Build the Kingdom, Night Wrestling,* and *Seduction of Lesser Gods*. She is a professor at Midland College in Texas.

Turning 60 proves the adage that happiness is an inside job. By 60, most of us have lived enough — through good times and bad — to know that material things and felicitous circumstances do not hold the key to how we feel inside. As Milton said in *Paradise Lost*, "The mind is its own place, and in itself can make a Heav'n of Hell, a Hell of Heav'n."

Sixty is a good time to start making a heaven of whatever hell we might still be in. Sixty is also a good time to step up the prayer life. After all, prayer is the only conversation we get to continue after we die, and it's nice to get to know in advance the person we will be spending eternity with.

I came by this tidbit of wisdom the hard way. Turning 40 was a traumatic experience. With a baby, a toddler, and an interminable Ph.D. program still unfinished, I caught the stomach bug my children had been passing back and forth — on top of an intestinal parasite we had already contracted from bottled water gone bad on the grocery shelves. As I hugged the toilet instead of eating cake, my prayer was for the time and energy to have a proper nervous breakdown.

The year I turned 50 was the best year of my life. The children had hit those preadolescent golden years, my marriage was happy, and I loved the students at the college where I taught (with a Ph.D. that turned out, after all, to be a terminal degree). My prayers were prayers of gratitude.

Then life took a nosedive, and I spent the early 50s in a midlife crisis so typical it was a living cliché. I floundered in my teaching career; suffered through a colonoscopy and a heart ablation; gave in to trifocals; and recovered, at last, from an abusive childhood — all the things the 50s are good for. (The only components missing were an affair and a red sports car.)

The kickoff for this midlife trauma was a broken rib cage. I spent six weeks immobile in an armchair by the window, praying for healing and survival. I learned some important things about prayer while I was stuck in that chair.

I learned that God does not always fix things, but He gives us a peace that really does pass understanding. Like toddlers in a circle at story time, we can scootch up close and listen really hard. When the going gets too difficult to bear, we can sit in His lap and let Him comfort us. Our lives may be in shambles, but He never denies His presence when we ask.

I've also learned that the only person I can change is me. The difficult people in my life are now free to be as obnoxious as they want. I will pray for them. If my (now grown) children didn't hear my advice the first 50,000 times I told them, they are now free to ignore it. I will pray for them as well. In fact, I have already started to spend more time praying than criticizing, and I've noticed a funny thing. I run into fewer and fewer grumpy people.

Hanging above my desk is a card that reads, "Faith is the confidence that God has your best interests in mind when He answers 'no' to your prayers." Learning this understanding has taken decades. Like my children who used to cry, "You don't love me!" when I denied their requests for candy, it's easy to believe God is withholding His love when He denies our requests. Yet God knows us better than we know ourselves, and at 60, we begin to realize that God is denying us the candy because He is preparing to serve us a hearty meal.

God always answers prayers. Sometimes the answer is "yes," sometimes "no," and sometimes "later." I'm never as excited about receiving "no" as about "yes," but at 60, I hope I'll be less whiny, knowing that a "no" often means "just wait, I have something even better in mind."

For Christians, life on Earth is preparation for Heaven (a kingdom we don't fully understand); lasting for eternity (a concept we can't conceive); serving a Lord (whose love is unfathomable). It's no wonder we feel that we are stumbling instead of gliding through life. Yet everything that happens to us here contributes to our readiness for the Kingdom of Heaven. That is the purpose of our time on Earth.

Our projects, our families, our friends, our circumstances, our joys, and our pain are all collected into the big basket we bring to Jesus' feet in prayer. Prayer is the answer to every question. Prayer is the basking in His love, the asking for forgiveness, the begging for His presence in times of difficulty, the offering up of our family and friends in need.

At 60, we know we will soon be facing the winter season of our lives. Potentially brutal, this final season also offers its own stark beauty if we're properly prepared. By

60, we wake up every morning with clear evidence that the body is a temporary structure, sighing and groaning into decay. Faster or slower, we will eventually be dust.

The most important part of turning 60 for me is a richer prayer life and a greater spiritual awareness, because, as exhilarating as this journey on Earth has been, home is a different destination.

15

Reflections on turning 60

At 60, the pace of life slows, but that allows time to experience things more deeply and understand them more profoundly.

By Rev. Kenneth W. Collier

Rev. Kenneth W. Collier is a retired minister of the Unitarian Society of Santa Barbara. He also served as Unitarian minister in Palo Alto and in several churches on the East Coast. Rev. Collier is a graduate of Starr King School for the Ministry in Berkeley and was ordained in 1979. In addition, he holds a Ph.D. in philosophy from the University of Pittsburgh. Ken has 3 daughters, one son, two stepsons, and 5 grandchildren.

Saturday I'll turn 60. Wow. How on earth did that happen? I'm finding it a funny feeling, turning 60. I've never had a birthday that was traumatic, and I don't expect this one to be. Still, I am finding it a bit different from the other 59. This is the first birthday that seems to mark a genuine boundary, an actual turning point in my life.

Always before, nothing much changed; I didn't feel any different from the way I had the day before. This time, though, I do feel different. I've been trying to figure out a good way to explain it. I'm not sure I can, but let me try. In the first place, I have noticed that the pace of my life seems to have slowed down. When I was younger, life seemed so urgent, so intensely time-bound. It seemed critical that so many things get done right away so that I could move on to the next new thing and the next thing and the next. The result was that I had a certain anxiety about living, a certain fear that I'd miss out on something or wouldn't get my due.

Things have changed. I've learned that very little is actually accomplished urgently, and I can wait for things to ripen. Mediocre wines can be drunk young, but there are no great wines that are not first barrel-aged and then bottle-aged, sometimes for years. Impatience can destroy a magnificent wine, and I've become more interested in drinking a few great wines than a lot of *vins ordinaires.* Life is just too short to waste it with impatience, and if that means that I'll miss out on some things, that there are things I'll never see or experience, well, then so be it.

Consider. I could rush through Florence, trying to see as much art as possible in the amount of time I have. Or, I could see fewer works, but spend the time with those that I do see to study them and experience them deeply. Truth be told, I'd rather miss Michelangelo's *David* entirely if it meant I'd have the time to begin to get a more profound understanding of his *Pietà*. And that's the metaphor. I'd rather have the years of life remaining to me to be deeper, even if it means I'll miss seeing the *David*. You just can't hurry depth.

Another thing that has happened over the last few years and seems somehow to be encapsulated for me in this coming birthday is that people are treating me differently now from the way they did even five years ago. I mentioned this in a sermon last spring. I'm no longer one of the Young Turk ministers. I was, back in my urgent days, but no longer. As I begin to revel in time, as I begin to reach deeper and can sit back and wait to see things develop, I've gained a certain perspective, a certain reflectiveness that I didn't used to have.

I know this may sound self-serving, but people listen to me differently from the way they used to. Maybe it's because, being more reflective and patient, I don't have such a chip on my shoulder, or maybe it's because I no longer need for my voice to be heard, especially not to be heard either first or last or loudest. I've become content to say what I have to say and listen to what others have to say. And that comes back to me as I am listened to — and disagreed with — in a different tone of voice, with a new level of respect.

Well, and what about those years that I do have left to me? I tease occasionally about how my life is now almost half over. The truth is, of course, none of us know how long we will live. Three score and ten? Maybe, but we've just celebrated a lot of four-score-and-ten-year-old-folks. So who knows. I'll live as long as I'll live, and that will have to be enough, especially since I have no choice in the matter! But when I consider the matter of my life ahead, I have two reactions. One, of course, is to let it ripen and to live in the only time we ever have, which is right now, this very moment. The other is to recognize that while it is, of course, true that all we have is this moment, it does not follow that planning is pointless. The formula I try to follow is to learn from the past, plan for the future, and live in the moment. So what about those future plans?

At the age of 60, of course, one almost inevitably begins to think about and plan for retirement, and I'm no exception. Of course I've begun to think about retiring, when and how and where. This should neither surprise nor dismay anyone. Now, the retirement of a minister is a little different from retirement in business in the same sorts of ways that a church is different from a business, even a nonprofit business.

I feel a lot like that old farmer who planted an orchard from which he would never harvest a single apple. When asked why he was planting it, he said two things. "First, I love this farm, and second, I want to pass it along to those who come after me." Well, I love this "farm," and I want to pass it along, healthy and strong, to those who follow me.

Serving as your minister has been, and continues to be, the culmination, the completion, the pinnacle of my career. I have never left a congregation less healthy than I found it, and so my intention is to move ahead over these last several years of my ministry with a deep commitment to whatever it takes to keep the society healthy, happy, and proud of all that we have accomplished together.

And these are my reflections as I turn 60.

Time

Yesterday is gone like the fragrance
Of a dream disappearing into sunlight,
And tomorrow is as unreal as the heat
Of a fire the lies in logs unkindled.

There is only this eternal moment,
As stationary as a star hanging golden
On the rich blue horizon, frozen
In the instant between sunset and evening.

It is a silent pane of glass that separates
The lost illusion of yesterday

From the unmade promise of tomorrow.

I watch the relentless flow of time
As promise passes into illusion,
And try to grasp this twinkling instant.

Section Three

GOOD VIBRATIONS

(The Beach Boys, 1966)

16

Go to where the art is

Discover what treasures may be hidden in your museum or art gallery.

by Faith Ringgold

Faith Ringgold is an acclaimed artist, writer, and professor emeritus at the University of California, San Diego where she taught art from 1984 until 2002. She is the recipient of more than 75 awards, including 18 Honorary Doctor of Fine Arts Degrees. Her art is included in many private and public art collections such as The Metropolitan Museum of Art, The National Museum of American Art, The Museum of Modern Art, and The Solomon R. Guggenheim Museum, among many others. Ringgold's first published book, *Tar Beach,* has won more than 30 awards including a Caldecott Honor Award and the Coretta Scott King award for the best illustrated children's book of 1991. Ms. Ringgold lives in Englewood, New Jersey and continues to support the talent, effort, dedication, and creativity of emerging artists.

We go to the cinema to see films, to the theater to see plays, to the concert hall to hear music, and to the museum to see art. If your work is to survive for the next generation, hearing about it by word of mouth is not good enough. It simply has to be seen, and the museum is the place for that. Rather than ignoring the power of museums, the informed public should make them accountable. You should go to museums and ask to see bought and exhibited the art you admire. No one group of people, no matter how rich or learned, can dictate the standards for quality in art. Only time and a cross section of informed viewers can ultimately determine the value and significance of the art of an era.

Along with many other artists of color and women, I now have the sweet good fortune of an audience of children who will grow up knowing that an artist does not have to be white or male. This alone will change the art world in the next decade. These young people will be our next artists, museum directors, curators, collectors, art critics, and teachers of art. They will be inspired by, collect, exhibit, and write about the art that they have learned as children to see as beautiful.

I have a story to tell you that is both a museum story and the best children's story I know — God bless them every one. Children all over the country tell me that when their parents bring them to New York they demand to be taken to the Guggenheim to see *Tar Beach.* How can I explain to children that museums often acquire works of art from collectors and yet never show them? (*Tar Beach* was bought by Judith Lieber, the pocketbook mogul, who then donated it to the Guggenheim in

1989.) So I said nothing and the children continued to go to the Guggenheim in search of *Tar Beach.*

Understandably, the personnel at the Guggenheim had never heard of *Tar Beach*; how could they possibly know the thousands of works of art in their permanent collection? But as the children continued to request to see *Tar Beach*, the personnel became annoyed with their persistence, and asked me why the kids thought it would be on view. I replied frankly that "I guess it is because they know *Tar Beach* is in your collection and they would like to see it on exhibition there." Finally, I received a letter from a museum administrator in which he wrote: "If you are not already aware, you should know that *Tar Beach* is currently one of, if not the most requested objects from our collection for loan to other institutions." But still, between you and me, I don't know what it would take to have this totally Eurocentric male-dominated Guggenheim Museum exhibit a painted story quilt by an African-American woman. So I don't hold my breath, but it was the innocence of children that initially broached the subject. And if *Tar Beach* ever hangs on the walls of the Guggenheim, it will be due to the children.

The issue of racism and sexism in the art world is a continuing problem that most people know very little about. Citizens don't demand equal rights for artists of color and women in museums and public funding agencies. Most people think if you're good enough, you'll make it to the top and so they don't urge their appointed officials to canvass the museums and other cultural institutions to see if they are spending public money to represent the best art done by artists regardless of race and sex.

Ninety-nine and nine-tenths percent of the significant art production of men and women of color is ignored by the major art institutions in this country and only token representation is given to the rest. I'd like to see that end — and it will. But right now the art world continues to have a field day and for the most part the only team players are white men.

Despite all of these obstacles, it has never occurred to me to stop, give up and go away — even though I know that is what oppression is designed to make me do. I continue to look for alternative routes to get where I want to be. That is why I have worked in so many different media: the posters, tankas, soft sculpture, and dolls in the 1970s; the performances and story quilts in the 1980s; and so far in the 1990s the writing and illustration of children's books, the rewriting of history in "The French Collection", and this autobiography. These things have given me a constantly expanding audience and the flexibility I need to continue working in the face of adversity.

Keep your sense of humor

A joke a day keeps the doctor away.

by Judy Brown

Judy Brown knows a good joke when she hears it. She was the comedy critic at the *L.A. Weekly* for more than a dozen years, and has contributed to the *Los Angeles Times*, the *New York Times* syndicate, and many other publications. She is the author of many joke collections, *The Comedy Thesaurus* and *Squeaky Clean Comedy.* Judy lives in Santa Monica, California.

Babies start to laugh at about four months of age and by the time a child reaches nursery school age, he or she will laugh 300 to 400 times a day (although I suspect at least 100 of those laughs are simply provoked by the word "doody").

However, by the time we're adults the laugh factor has dwindled down to a measly 10 to 15 times a day. A sorry situation indeed, although it may be due to the development of a more sophisticated and discerning sense of humor (the "doody" joke having worn thin for many of us).

But I believe that this humor deficit can also be credited to the thoroughly adult occupation of having to hold down a freakin' job, instead of having the time to dissolve into chuckles whenever a playmate fingerpaints with brownish colors. But at 60, we're approaching the age when we can kiss the boss goodbye (especially if our planned retirement includes a sexual harassment suit).

I believe we're entering a new jolly time of life, when we can devote ourselves to more pleasurable pursuits such as laughter. And depending on the individual's mental acuity and physical dexterity, perhaps also a return to paint applied with fingers. We're also at an age when many of us have grandchildren, which means we can share laughter with our adorable blood-relative toddlers at that joint target: their parents. And there's no reason we shouldn't beat the tittering little tykes in volume chuckles on our own laughmentum.

Philosopher John Morreall theorized that human laughter may have its biological origins as a kind of shared expression of relief at the passing of danger. By simply surviving to age 60, we've banked thousands of past dangers at which we all can now laugh with relief, including (but not limited to): mutual funds in the 1970s (and '90s), Republican administrations, and pregnancy scares.

However, at 60 we're also looking forward to the built-in dangers that come with age itself; which, in my opinion, laughter has as much potential to fight as stem cell research does to piss off fundamentalists.

Laughter can keep you young, or at the very least, alive. Research indicates that, after exposure to humor, there's a general increase in activity within your immune system and a decrease in stress hormones.

Also, according to William Fry, M.D., a leading expert on humor and health, a good belly laugh speeds up the heart rate, improves blood circulation and works muscles all over the body. "It's an aerobic exercise," he's said.

Laughter, in fact, is my favorite form of workout: one that can be done sitting down, while drinking a strawberry margarita.

To facilitate your humor exercises and continued hilarious health in your golden giggle years, Dr. Judy here has written a prescription: a book which compiles the best material from stand-up comedians that address the subject; it's called: *Getting Old is a Joke.*

Herewith, some free samples. Have a laugh (or three) on me:

You know you've reached middle age when you're cautioned to slow down by your doctor, instead of by the police.

Joan Rivers

They say aging is a funny thing, but there's nothing funny about it. You still feel 14, but when you turn on the bathroom light, this ugly old guy in the mirror leaps out at you.

Eric Idle

I didn't realize I was getting old until my attorney advised me to get my affairs in order. Okay, so now I have Andy on Monday, Bob on Tuesday, and the FedEx man on Wednesday.

Katherine Poehlmann

I remember my own dear grandfather. He smoked and drank every day of his life until he was 81. Then we had to kill him.

Roseanne Barr

God bless my mom, she had reverse Alzheimer's. Towards the end she remembered everything, and she was pissed.

S. Rachel Lovey

You can live to be a hundred if you give up all the things that make you want to live to be a hundred.

Woody Allen

The nicest thing about being in my 60s is that I know I'm not going to die in my 50s.

Bill Wiggins

18

Go ahead and inhale

Yoga is just what the doctor ordered for aging boomers. So sit back, take stock, flex your muscles, catch your breath, and get on with your life!

by Alice Waldman

Alice Waldman cofounded the Shaki Yoga Center in Staten Island, N.Y., in her late 50s. She offers classes in hatha yoga, meditation, and yoga philosophy there and through community outreach programs with Staten Island University Hospital, the National Park Service, the Eden School for Autistic Children and Adults, and the Staten Island Historical Society.

First and foremost, yoga is a practice, not a competitive sport. So no matter what physical condition you are in, there are yoga poses you can do. And no matter how long you have been practicing or how masterful you are, there is always more to learn — and there are deeper, subtler levels to reach.

I tried yoga in my younger days, but never stuck with it. Finally, when I was 54 years old, I tried it again — and got hooked. What a wonderful addiction it is! No matter how I am feeling, I can always count on feeling better, after practicing.

Over the past several years, yoga has become "mainstream." Young, skinny supermodels in yoga poses advertise everything from feminine-hygiene products to luxury vacations. Celebrities, twisted into pretzel-like shapes, are featured on magazine covers. All forms of media continue to hype the amazing benefits of yoga.

As a matter of fact, all of these claims are true. Yoga has been shown to counteract stress, reduce high blood pressure, relieve migraine headaches, alleviate back pain, the list goes on and on. It is especially beneficial for 60-plus folks — helping us maintain flexibility, muscle tone, bone density, energy, and overall health. It is also true that anyone can do yoga. You don't have to be young, slim, fit, or flexible. It is never too late to start; you will reap yoga's benefits from Day One.

How do you begin? The principle elements of a yoga practice are: breathing, physical postures, deep relaxation, and meditation.

Step One: Master your breathing.
Even if you are ill or bedridden, breathing fully will help you feel better and increase your energy level. The most

basic of the yogic breathing techniques is the Three-part Breath. To familiarize yourself with this technique, it helps to concentrate on one part at a time.

1) Take a comfortable seated position, either on the floor or in a straight-backed chair. Place a hand over your belly button. Inhale through your nose, all the way to the bottom of your lungs, allowing the breath to puff out your belly. Then, exhale through your nose, and at the end of the exhalation, draw your belly in gently toward your spine — to completely empty out your lungs. Repeat a few times, to achieve a smooth rhythm.

2) Place your hands on either side of your rib cage. Inhaling through your nose, allow your belly to puff out, then lift and expand your rib cage into your hands. Exhaling through your nose, contract your belly toward the spine and allow your ribs to move down, and away, from your hands. Repeat these two parts several times, to get the hang of it.

3) Place one hand at the top of your chest, over the hollow between your collarbones. Inhaling through your nose, puff out your belly, expand your rib cage, and bring the breath to your hand — to softly lift and open the upper chest. Exhaling through your nose, draw in the belly, allow the rib cage to drop and contract, and finally soften the upper chest away from your hand.

Now, put it all together: Rest your hands on your legs, close your eyes, and practice — working toward a rhythmic pattern where the inhalation and exhalation are of equal length. Repeat this for several minutes and you will feel both relaxed and energized.

Step Two: Strike a pose.

There are dozens of basic yoga poses — with variations, the total number climbs into the thousands. They are designed to move the body in all the directions it is capable of — forward, backward, side to side, twisting, standing, sitting, prone, supine, upright, and upside down — and also to massage and stimulate your internal organs and regulate your endocrine system. Striking just a few simple poses will stretch and open your body, and get your energy moving freely.

Mountain Pose: Stand with your feet a hip-width apart, and parallel. Press your feet firmly into the floor and lift your arms toward the sky — with the palms facing each other and the elbow, wrists, and fingers straight. Simultaneously, drop your shoulder blades down your back — so that you don't scrunch your neck. Hold this position for several breaths, allowing each inhalation to help you lengthen through your torso and each exhalation to help you relax into the pose. Lower your arms back down to your sides. This will strengthen your legs, improve your posture, and energize you.

Bridge Pose: Lie down on your back, on the floor. Bend your knees, placing both feet on the floor a hip-width apart — so that your ankles are directly under your knees. Rest your arms by your sides, with palms facing the floor. Pressing into your feet and your arms, lift your back off the floor. Press down through the back of your head and the mounds of your big toes. Extend your tail-bone toward your knees. Draw the bottom tips of your shoulder blades toward your spine — to help open and expand your heart. Hold this pose for several breaths, then slowly release to the floor. Bend your knees into your chest and hug your legs.

Congratulations! You have stretched your chest, neck, and spine; stimulated your abdominal organs, lungs, and thyroid; rejuvenated tired legs; improved digestion; alleviated stress; and calmed brain activity. Now, wasn't that worth the work?

Modified Knee-down Twist: Remaining on your back, bend your knees and place both feet on the floor, with your big-toe joints touching. Stretch your arms out at shoulder height — so that you are in the shape of a "T." As you exhale, drop both knees to the floor on your right and turn your head to look at your left fingers. Hold this for a few breaths, feeling your body stretch diagonally — from your right shoulder blade to your kneecaps. On an exhalation, unwind gently back to the center. Take two full breaths, then repeat on the other side. This will massage your liver and kidneys; stretch your shoulders, hips, and neck; energize your spine; and stimulate your digestive system.

Step Three: Time to relax!

Never, ever, cheat yourself out of relaxation! The time spent relaxing helps your body to integrate the work you have been doing. Lie down on your back, in "corpse pose," with your legs slightly separated and your feet relaxed. Rest your arms a few inches away from your sides, palms facing up. Close your eyes and let your body melt into the floor. Realize that you are fully supported, and you don't need to do anything but let the Earth hold you.

Now, deepen your breath, bend your knees, and roll over onto your right side. Using your left hand to push up, come to a seated position. Close your eyes and draw your inner gaze to your third eye — the space between your eyebrows. Bring your attention to your breath and enjoy a few moments of quiet meditation.

The next time you go out into the world, you may wonder why everyone else seems to be rushing and so stressed out. Revel in the peace and calmness that comes with yoga practice. Appreciate yourself, respect your body, embrace your friends and family. Spread the joy!

19

Ask the big questions

In your sixth decade, it's time to search within to find your inner wisdom. Striving to understand why you're here can ease anxiety, anger, and fear, and move you toward life-affirming action!

by Tina B. Tessina, Ph.D.

Tina B. Tessina, Ph.D. (www.tinatessina.com), is a licensed psychotherapist in Southern California with experience in counseling individuals and couples. She is the author of 14 books, including *It Ends with You: Grow Up and Out of Dysfunction,* and publishes the *Happiness Tips from Tina* e-mail newsletter. Dr. Tessina is an online relationships expert, "Psychology Smarts" columnist for *First for Women*, and has appeared on radio and TV.

Perhaps the most important lesson I've learned is that a meaningful life is about growing your soul — and it happens slowly, in the process of engaging life.

My own soul was battered early when my whole family died during my teenage years, and I was left alone, terrified, without money, education, or an idea of what to do. I just stumbled through the days, months, and years, too afraid to feel what I feared was inside me, grasping at the wrong lifelines and clinging to the wrong people until, divorced, bereft, suicidal, and single, at age 27, I entered therapy and began to develop my soul through exploring my feelings. This decision saved my life and became the basis for a personal renaissance. As I searched for meaning and purpose, I began to understand I'd been put on Earth to learn and grow, and to use what I'd learned in the process of healing myself to help others. Now that I've just turned 62, I find that sense of purpose is still serving me well and has been the source of many blessings.

As a child with no religious training, but growing up in the beautiful surroundings of the Catskill Mountains, I sensed a Power behind the workings of the Universe, which has inspired me to yearn and aspire, comforted me in times of pain, and provided clarity and direction when I needed it. Human relationships bruise, batter, and comfort me, and teach resilience and humility. Love urges my soul to blossom and grow; compassion causes it to blur at the edges. And so I learn to accept others as they are.

Every day, I have the delight and privilege of loving Richard, my husband, a real, human, fallible man. My friends are an equal blessing and challenge. We can be cranky, we occasionally hurt each other's feelings, and we don't always say the right thing. But we are here for each other when we're really needed, we do our best to be caring and kind, and we forgive each other's imperfections.

Most of my clients come to me, not searching for the meaning of life, but focused on some crisis in their lives: a relationship disaster; marriage or family problems; lack of direction and motivation; some huge loss for which they're grieving; an emotional problem, such as anxiety or depression; or perhaps for help in recovering from an addiction. As we sort through the crisis, handle immediate problems, and get everything settled down, and then embark on an extended process of figuring out what happened and what must change, their life gets easier.

Then, frequently, a patient asks: "Now that I'm in charge of myself and have a lot of extra energy, and life is a lot easier and my relationships are working, it feels like I'm missing something. The question is: *What am I doing here?*"

Once the basics of life are established and understood, many people need a sense of meaning and a higher sense of purpose than just survival. When self-confidence and self-esteem are in place, we need a challenge to feel satisfied, a way to express our uniqueness and individuality — to ourselves, to friends, and to the world.

If your life's purpose is not evident to you already, how do you find out what it is? Where does a sense of purpose come from? It comes from within and cannot be imposed or chosen from outside. Your purpose may be your livelihood, or it may have nothing to do with how you make a living. Your purpose may be a simple one, like making a good, healthy life for yourself and your children, or it may be more dramatic and based on what you've learned by healing your own childhood experience. Inner purpose has the power to transform anxiety, anger, fear, and rage into powerful, life-affirming action. A life's purpose gives you the means to control your destiny, no matter what the force of the hardships you have incurred.

Most of the world's spiritual thinkers agree that we all have the the wisdom to guide each of us — if we just know how to listen and to trust what we learn. Purpose may make itself clear in one instant flash, or gradually — by following clues, one at a time. Whether you get insight all at once or a piece at a time, work and experience are required to nurture it. Inner wisdom is not rational or practical in nature, but intuitive and spiritual. It can provide a way to see the big picture, or a more detached and objective viewpoint of the issues and problems of life. Each new idea must be tested through practical use to see how it works. Step by step, using both intuitive wisdom and clear thinking, you can bring your inner motivation to the surface and use it to create what you want. Inspiration expressed through action will develop the meaning of your own life.

Here's how I expressed my own life experience, in a poem called "Grace":

Life
is worked
On a wheel
Sloppy, slippery
Formless base clay
Rising coaxed, caressed,
Coerced and beaten into shape
Tested in passion's consuming fire
Until worthy to catch and hold
A bit of the liquid grace
Pouring unceasingly over us.

Chill out and meditate

Who hasn't wanted to escape to a tropical island — to rest, relax, rejuvenate? You won't need a magic carpet to get away! Just close your eyes — and meditate!

by Joan Goldstein

Joan Goldstein studied yoga in India under the guidance of a master and began teaching meditation in the 1980s. Co-author, with Manuela Soares, of *The Joy Within*, she created a unique corporate training program in stress management at Home Insurance in 1993. Ms. Goldstein currently teaches meditation classes at the Karpas Health Center at Beth Israel Hospital in New York.

I'm talking about meditation — your passport to peace of mind. And it is a kind of magic. How would you like to drop some of those 60 years? When you meditate, you can be 60, or 30, or a child. The years disappear, you tap into the energy of the universe, and become ageless.

And there's an added bonus. When you drop those years, you'll also drop all that noisy chatter in the background. I'm talking about the parade of thoughts that march through your mind every day. Your ego fuels some of it. You're very important to yourself, of course, and you can sometimes get red-hot mad about the things people say to you. The result? You carry these angry thoughts with you all day.

It's all bad baggage — a pollution of the mind that you need to release. Meditation helps you do this. It can lower your blood pressure, relieve stress, reduce fatigue, and clear up your thinking. Is it any wonder that doctors are beginning to sing its praises?

If you've been curious about meditation but have been put off — because it seems like some kind of mumbo jumbo, I want to tell you that it's not. And you've already got all the tools you'll need, inside of you.

Getting started

Never meditated before and wondering how to begin? Sit in on a class! Tapping into the energy in a class will give you a quick boost. You'll also pick up valuable tips and guidelines to help you meditate by yourself. For meditation, even in a class, is something for you — and you alone.

I usually advise people to set aside ten minutes a day to meditate — right before bedtime, if possible. It will help you unwind and allow you to have a refreshing sleep — so that you'll feel energized in the morning.

You can meditate any time of day, though — even on a lunch break. Search out a quiet spot in your office, or maybe on a park bench, and begin. Here are a few simple rules:

1) Whether sitting in a chair or on the floor, keep your back straight, but not rigid. Rest one hand in the other, on your lap. (You might also try this lying on your back.)

2) Close your eyes and let your mind follow your breath — as you breathe in and breathe out.

3) Breathe the way you naturally breathe. With each inhalation, repeat silently to yourself, "Breathing in." With each exhalation, repeat, "Breathing out." Keep your mind focused on your breath. If there's a distracting noise in the background, don't struggle to block it out. Simply acknowledge it; say, "Hearing," and bring your attention back to your breath.

4) Do this for ten minutes. At the end of this time, you'll find that the anger, fear, and other frustrations that have built up during the day have faded into the background, and you've taken in the healing energy around

you. You'll feel relaxed and rejuvenated. In fact, it's a good idea to do this with a stopwatch or a timer, or you may fall asleep — that's how relaxed you'll be!

On weekends, when you have more time and the weather permits, consider meditating outdoors. Henry Miller said: "The moment one gives close attention to anything, even a blade of grass, it becomes a mysterious, awesome, indescribably magnificent world in itself." I know this is true because I've experienced it so many times myself. One day, when I was meditating outdoors, the first thing I saw when I opened my eyes was a tree blooming with its first green leaves of the season, and some flowers — beautiful yellow pansies with their faces upturned, as though they were smiling at me. My heart opened up to the beauty of nature! It was wonderful; I really had tapped into the joy within me.

Choosing your mantra

In Sanskrit, mantra means "that which protects." Think of a mantra as a mystical and powerful formula handed down to us through the ages by sages and seers in deep meditation. In particularly tense, stressful times, a mantra can help to soothe and calm you.

You can be given a mantra in a class, or you can pick up a tape on meditation at any bookstore and choose a mantra. I'll tell you a story: One of my students had her wallet stolen while she was on vacation. She called home to see if anyone had tried to contact her about her missing wallet and while she was listening to her messages, got one from herself. It seems that she previously had called her machine and recorded her mantra, and some of the chants we had done in class. Almost unconsciously, she began to repeat her mantra and the chants to herself. Gradually, she felt herself coming down from her terribly agitated state, and relaxed.

A mantra will do that. Meditation will do that. Try it — and you'll open up a whole new world for yourself. I did!

21

Leave a legacy of care

A defining moment for a child inspired a lifelong passion for all things wild. Now, this champion of conservation medicine offers advice on how to care for the Earth even after you leave it.

By Mary Pearl

Mary Pearl is the former president of Wildlife Trust and cofounder of the Consortium for Conservation Medicine. She served as editor of the series, "Methods and Cases in Conservation Science," and coeditor of *Conservation Medicine: Ecological Health in Practice*, the first edited volume on the field, which explores the links among the ecosystem, wildlife, and human health. She is the current Dean of William E. Macaulay Honors College.

As a small child, I spent a lot of time in the open spaces and woods in the suburb where I was raised. One memorable morning when I was about five, as my friend Billy McAndrew and I were exploring the neighborhood, we discovered on the ground, in a little nook between two pickets of a white fence, three baby cottontails. Children notice things, especially things close to the ground. I'll never forget that discovery, nor the pleasure I took in those days trying to walk as silently as I could so that I could see and hear as much of nature as possible. That was how I became a naturalist.

Many adults probably remember similar childhood encounters with nature, in those unhurried days when no one thought it unproductive for youngsters to wander about, splashing in puddles or turning up the leaf litter with a stick. Then came the moment when it was time to prepare for adult lives and assume the responsibilities of the workplace and family.

Now that the years of juggling childrearing, caring for parents, and climbing the career ladder are drawing to a close, we have the opportunity once again to savor nature. I've compiled a list of ways that we may reclaim our naturalist pasts, which includes walks, readings, and quiet meditations in wild places, sharing your appreciation with others, or even creating a conservation easement for your property so that others like you may enjoy the tranquility of open spaces long after you are gone.

- ***Take the time to explore the natural landscapes where you live.*** You'll probably have to go to a state park or some other kind of protected area rather than the end of the road where you live, but fortunately, parks are abundant in our country. While everyone else is sitting in traffic on a gorgeous morning, you can be kayaking on a lake bordered by trees displaying every shade of green imaginable. Walk silently along the nature trails. It never ceases to amaze me how few people venture more than a few yards from a parking lot. Even in the summer, hiking trails can offer solitude and opportunities to appreciate wild flowers, birds, insects, and even the occasional reptile or mammal.

Winter is even more fun. Now is the time to invest in a pair of snowshoes: while younger people revel in speeding down the ski slopes, you can investigate the secrets of the forests at an appropriately slow pace. On snowshoes one day after a snowstorm, I was able to deduce by the lack of footprints and the presence of droppings next to a tree that a giant flying squirrel lived in the branches above. Even though I was a biologist studying monkeys in the Himalayan foothills, I had not known until that moment that this very large animal made its home in a tree near my house.

If snowshoeing is not your idea of pleasure, a visit to the zoo in winter is always rewarding. The animals that thrive outdoors are friskier and more beautiful in their thickened fur coats. Indoors, the moist, warm air of the exhibits of animals from warmer climates can transport you to the tropics.

• ***Now is the time to reread Thoreau.*** Along with descriptions of nature are also hilarious descriptions of people. While hiking the length of Cape Cod, for example, he noted that the local people were "well preserved," elaborating that the women there were "dessicated" and the men "pickled." Thoreau, John Muir, Rachel Carson, and other nature writers remind us, usually in more positive ways, how much the American character is formed by our natural environment.

Looking forward, how much of your grandchildren's character will be formed by experiences in the outdoors? E. O. Wilson has written that people have a natural appreciation for nature, called "biophilia," which serves us well because it causes us to want the healthy ecosystems — characterized by abundant and diverse life forms — that are the basis of our own well-being. Yet people cannot love what they cannot see or understand. Therefore, if you want to leave a legacy of respect for the environment, it is important not only to experience nature yourself, but to ensure that those who follow will do the same.

• ***Create a legacy of concern for nature.*** There are many ways to encourage others to value wildlife. By volunteering as a docent at your favorite zoo, botanical garden, or nature center, you can teach children about the importance of conservation. For many children, this informal education can instill a love of nature and also of science as a way of knowing about the world around them.

Your impact can be enormous. More people go to zoos each year than go to all sporting events *combined.* Don't feel comfortable around kids? Understaffed parks everywhere can use help in maintaining trails and picnic areas.

If you are a gardener, you already spend a considerable amount of time outside. No one wants the insect pests that attack cultivated plants, but now you have more time to consider ways of controlling pests that do not involve heavy use of pesticides. Learn more about organic gardening. Gardens with greater diversity of plants, especially native plants, have less severe pest infestations. Consider transforming at least a portion of your yard into a habitat of native plants, and enjoy the increase in birds and butterflies that visit your garden. If you live in a more rural area, be sure to maintain corridors of brush and trees that can provide safe passage for wildlife moving from one stand of forest to another.

If you are fortunate enough to live on a beautiful, extensive property, consider protecting it from being ruined one day. Instead of becoming a future housing development or series of "ranchettes," the land can be protected forever through a legal device known as a *conservation easement.* Even if the land is sold, it can never be broken up into small bits or turned into a shopping center.

Talk to a lawyer about this way of ensuring that future generations of children can walk along the land and suddenly find themselves in front of a little warren of cottontail babies.

Be inspired night and day

Through the years, you may have focused on maintaining a career, raising children, and running a household. You weren't so much inspired as compelled, driven, required. Now, becoming 60 may mean that these obligations are receding, leaving room to investigate other pursuits.

by Greg Mort

Greg Mort grew up during the height of the Space Race between Russia and the United States. When he was five, his father took him outside to gaze into a star-filled sky to observe Sputnik, the world's first artificial satellite. That event helped shape his life's vocation and avocation. Now, as a professional artist with works in prominent museum and private collections around the world, Mr. Mort melds his passions for art and astronomy into one flowing stream.

Inspiration. I am convinced that the very fabric of art and astronomy are imbedded in our DNA, part and parcel of the human existence. Have you felt this pull also? When you view a sculpture or painting, do you feel yourself strangely bonded to its artist? And, like me, as you gaze at the night sky, do you get the feeling that it claims *you* for its own?

I'll admit that I'm a passionate seeker of beauty, in both art and the stars. For as long as I can remember, painting and astronomy have sustained and fulfilled me on a daily basis. In fact, I'll wager that if you locked me up in a room that lacked paints and windows, it wouldn't take long for my soul to go into painful withdrawal.

I submit that artistic yearning and expression evolves from our need to bond with this great universe, to leave a bit of our essence behind when we ourselves join the stars. I paint to leave a bit of my soul, guided by the creative pulse of the artists who came before me.

Let me put this another way. Who among us is not lured by the sight and warmth of a fire? And why, after 40,000 generations, do we still feel a kind of hypnotic quality in those flames? The reason is simple. It's because for 99 percent of our history we huddled around those fires. They represented security, light, heat, a way of staying alive. Though our technological advances long ago made this way of keeping warm obsolete, the fascination of the flames remains.

Why? Because they are part of our collective human experience. The same holds true for human creativity.

Like those early artists who felt the inclination to draw on cave walls, I also feel the need to capture what I see.

It's been said that artists are born, not made. Perhaps. Perhaps not. Maybe I paint better than you because I've given myself permission to plug into the creative pulse I feel so strongly.

Were you, perhaps, told by your parents that you weren't creative, or did you take it to heart when a well-meaning art "teacher" cautioned you to "stay within the lines"? It's a good thing Walt Disney ignored the teacher who admonished him that flowers shouldn't have faces! Disney gave the world considerable beauty and inspiration — because he drew from the fount of universal creativity.

Now that you're in your 60s, old enough to care little about what others think, and old enough to make your own rules, perhaps you'll give yourself permission to create your own art.

The good news is that artistic expression is not difficult to access once you decide to tap into it. And once you connect, you'll become an addict like me. You won't be able to resist the infusion of invigoration and renewal, the high of birthing a form that only you can create.

A visit to an art museum is a great place to discover artistic inspiration. There, you can connect with various forms of art on its most intimate terms. Perhaps it is the texture and glisten of the paint, or the dimensionality of the piece that grabs my soul, but I leave itching to paint.

The world's great monuments also serve to inspire. To behold the menagerie of animals drawn on the cave walls of Lascaux is to bear witness to some of the most expressive works ever created by human hands. The paintings tell of the spirit of the hunt, but the quarry represents much more than food. The paintings were a means of connecting with the spirit of the creatures themselves. In essence, the artists were paying homage to Earth's bounty while praising the majesty of the Universe.

Similarly, the sheer size and mass of the stone markers at Stonehenge, the mysterious astronomical sculpture on the Salisbury plain in England, attest to the ancients' desire to connect with the stars, a universe so expansive it makes the massive stones seem like pebbles.

On the days when I need a huge infusion of creative inspiration, however, I head for the stars. There are few things I savor more than venturing from the glare of city lights to slip into the refuge of a moonless night sky. Shhhhh, I tell my soul: be still, be quiet.

There, under the canopy of a starry blanket, I am overcome, humbled, by the vastness of the Universe. Yet, I am comforted by the knowledge that I am tied to it. I sigh in contentment, knowing I have seen this lightshow before — perhaps even a million years ago. Listening, I can distinctly make out the tick-tock of the clockwork of the heavens and its ever-flowing creative hum.

When I view original art, be it a painting or a starry star, I instinctively feel close to its maker.

This knowledge awaits you, too. If you're in the city, jump into your car this very night and drive until you find a perfect spot clear enough for stargazing. Or, jump on a plane and take in the majesty of Stonehenge, perhaps on the longest day of the year, as the sun rises between two of the monoliths. Your soul will connect with the Universe; its beauty will bring you home.

23

Fall in love

Two people with respectable jobs, both parents of grown children, meet, fall in love, then together they fall in love again with the improbable and mystical world of classical Chinese medicine. Along the way, they discover each other and a new way of life and retirement-free careers.

by Fran Maher and Brian Coffey

Fran Maher and Brian Coffey have been practicing Chinese medicine in central New Jersey for more than a decade. They thank their many generous Chinese teachers for their training. Both are graduates of Nanjing University of Traditional Chinese Medicine. Ms. Maher is a New Jersey licensed acupuncturist. Mr. Coffey is a licensed massage therapist specializing in clinical qi gong.

When I was 50-something, I fell in love with a man who practiced Chinese esoteric arts that include internal martial art and qi gong, an ancient Chinese health modality. I had already been a practioner of the Sufi esoteric tradition for about 20 years — whirling, dancing, slow hypnotic movements, and chanting. Not every day, but over a period of years I studied and I learned. During this time, I also had become interested in health foods as well as becoming a collector of folk and home remedies for just about everything that can befall a human being; I'd fallen in love with good health.

Outwardly, my life did not appear esoteric. I had (and still have) a split-level home in the suburbs, a respectable job in the world of business, and three pretty much grown-up kids. (Hang in there, it's going to take a little while to get to the 60 part, because I wasn't born yesterday.)

So I met this man, and our esoteric interests converged. One of his tai chi buddies had told him about a Sufi session he had attended and mentioned belly dancing. (Of course, not everything is esoteric.) So this guy showed up and joined the class. Afterward, the teacher and the class participants cooked a big vegetarian meal. "Oh," my new friend said, upon finding out that I'm pretty much a vegetarian all the time. "I've always wanted to try a vegetarian diet."

Part of me thought that this was a line, and part of me didn't care because he was about the cutest thing I'd seen walk through the Sufi door.

We carpooled to a few more Sufi classes. I remained skeptical about him, until a few weeks later he showed me a technique he had learned from a Chinese qi gong teacher, a method to send a soft, subtle lightening out of the palms of his hands. Qi gong (say "chee gong") is a system of still and movement meditations to balance the energy of the body. I said, "Do you think I'd be able to feel it if you aimed it at me?"

Turned out that I could feel it. In fact, with my eyes closed, ten out of ten times I could describe exactly where his hands were near me, emitting this warm glow. So we went for 100 out of 100 or so. Besides, he could dance the cha-cha, something you didn't have a chance to learn where I grew up in the Midwest.

Other stuff, too. And we laughed together. Oh, how we laughed; joyous, happy, and silly. (Believe me, I'm getting closer to the 60 part.)

Brian (that's his name) taught me how to create the glow from my hands, too, and we discovered by experimenting on ourselves and every family member who would hold still long enough that sending the glow toward another person could speed his or her healing.

In almost the same breath, we fell in love with the idea of helping others feel better. Brian quit his perfectly respectable business job and went to massage school to begin to learn more about anatomy and the human body. We got married. My mother, who was hoping he was still a New York executive, was aghast. One day, driving home from a visit to Sufi camp, we found a magazine, *Qi Journal*, in a health food store. One of the articles described what we were doing as the healing aspect of qi gong, and an ancient part of Chinese medicine. We wept with wonder and excitement. In that same issue we found a small ad placed by a man who taught "Chinese healing arts." We went to see him.

What we learned from him was a type of health care that is approximately 8,000 years old. We learned how to do it in a way that is effective and safe and teachable. After awhile, our teacher authorized us to teach it to others on behalf of his small school. And we fell in love with it all, including the teacher. However, Brian had a massage therapy license and I had a driver's license so at the brink of 60 (we finally got to 60!), I decided to go for acupuncture accreditation. That meant acupuncture school. Brian came, too, to learn and to keep me company.

My accountant, friends, and other people who look out for me just in case I get too flaky said, "Why are you doing this at your age? Education is an investment. You'll never even make your tuition back, let alone earn a living!" But we take this with a grain of salt, because they are also the people who said, "Why are you getting married? Just live together. You'll get more Social Security." I don't know how to answer them. Maybe this essay is my answer.

By the time we graduated, Brian was 60, too. He turned 60 in China, the fifth anniversary of his dragon birth year. Dragons were everywhere. We were there on internships at a hospital in Nanjing, learning traditional Chinese medicine. We fell in love with China. Brian decided that the discipline of acupuncture school had helped his qi gong and that his practice and teaching path would continue to be qi gong, but I still faced national boards and license exams.

I never did fall in love with exams and tests. But I had broken my arm and couldn't sleep nights, so I spent the time meditating and studying. Even when I had accomplished my credentials, I wasn't sure I'd like practicing acupuncture — but guess what? I fell in love with the clinical work and with all the people who come for help with their health issues. I guess this is where I've been heading all my life. And from here, it looks like a retirement-free career.

So what did I learn? I learned a lot at 40, more so at 50, and to an even greater extent at 60 — I learned to follow my heart. Do you think that will be true at 70? Brian and I believe it will be true for us as long as we live.

You follow your heart, too, and let yourself fall in love, and fall in love again.

PAPA'S GOT A BRAND NEW BAG

(James Brown, 1965)

24

Live to 100!

You could live another 40 years. All it takes are healthy doses of optimism, good genes, exercises for the body and the brain, and a weight-conscious diet. No smoking or quack remedies allowed.

by Thomas T. Perls M.D., M.P.H., F.A.C.P.

Dr. Thomas T. Perls completed his training in Internal Medicine at Harbor-UCLA Medical Center in Torrance, California, and in Geriatrics at Harvard Medical School and Mount Royal Hospital in Melbourne, Australia. The founder and director of the NIH-funded New England Centenarian Study, the largest study of centenarians and their families in the world, Dr. Perls is the author of the award-winning book *Living to 100, Lessons in Maximizing Your Health At Any Age.*

I've studied centenarians now for more than 12 years. These are people, mind you, who have lived at least 40 more years beyond the age of 60. A current centenarian was 60 years old in 1960. Whoever thought when people turned 60 that they might have the years, equivalent of a whole other adulthood ahead of them! But now, centenarians are the fastest-growing segment of our population, and we so frequently hear about them that they raise the bar for the rest of us in terms of what life expectancies we see for ourselves.

What life expectancy should we expect? The Seventh Day Adventist Health Study reveals that most of us should be able to live to our mid-to-late 80s. Following the rules of their religion, Seventh Day Adventists are vegetarian and regularly exercise, don't smoke, and don't drink alcohol. (Though, perhaps drinking a bit of alcohol every day is good for you.) In addition, their weekends are dedicated to their faith and family. Perhaps the emphasis upon faith and family allows these people to effectively manage their stress. The result of these behaviors is that the Adventists have the longest average life expectancy in the world at approximately 88 years.

Unlike the Adventists, however, average life expectancy for most people in industrialized nations is currently 77 years or ten years less. The reasons are not difficult to guess. Over 70 percent of Americans are overweight; 30 percent of these are obese; people still smoke cigarettes; only 15 percent of people regularly exercise; and diets that promote obesity, heart attacks, strokes, diabetes, and cancer are prevalent. As a Scandinavian twins' study points out, the vast majority of how old people can live is determined by their health-related behaviors. What's more, the New England Centenarian

Study noted that close to 90 percent of centenarians were independently functioning at the average age of 92 years, thus compressing the time that they aren't well toward the end of their exceptionally long lives. The centenarians thus show us that it is not a matter of "the older you get, the sicker you get," but rather, "the older you get, the healthier you've been." This empowering and optimistic view very likely applies to anyone who can come close to achieving the lifespan his/her body and environment are built for. No longer should we assume that life after 60 is a downhill slide. Instead, most people should be able to live nearly 30 additional years, most of that time independently. Good health habits are the prerequisite.

So what are the good health habits or characteristics that help people maximize their life expectancy and the time that they are healthy? The acronym AGEING (the British spelling of aging) will help you remember some of the most important points.

Attitude. Centenarians tend to be funny, gregarious, and optimistic. They manage their stress, shedding it, instead of internalizing it. Thus, attempt to acquire a centenarian attitude.

Genetics. While you can't change your genes, you certainly can learn from them. Assess the longevity in your family. Do relatives generally die in their 90s and older? Or do they die in their 60s or 70s? If the former, that is wonderful news for you. Longevity runs very strongly in families. Perhaps you can even indulge a bit in not so healthy habits, but only once in awhile! On the other hand, if relatives generally die in their 60s and 70s, alarm bells should be going off. It is very important that you participate in a diligent program of prevention and screening so that you either prevent or catch problems before they catch you.

Exercise. Exercise 30 minutes a day, at least five days a week. And, as you get older, weight lifting (strength training) becomes all the more important to regain and prevent muscle loss. Muscle doesn't just keep you strong and help with your balance and prevent falls. Increasing your muscle mass prevents osteoporosis (bone loss and fractures), improves sleep, burns fat, and can even help your memory. You can build muscle at any age.

Interests. Just as it is important to exercise your different muscles, it is also important to exercise different parts of your brain. To do this, take on new cognitive activities that you haven't performed before. For example, bridge, Scrabble, or Sudoku. The most powerful activities are learning a new language or musical instrument. Once you become good at the activity, move on to something new and difficult. Exercising your brain, at any age, can delay the onset or progression of memory loss and other cognitive problems that can be associated with aging.

Nutrition. The most important point about nutrition is to be on a diet that helps you maintain a healthy weight. Obesity is strongly associated with most age-related diseases. It is wise to stay away from sweets, minimize red meat in your diet, and keep an eye on your total number of calories per day.

Get rid of smoking and quackery. Smoking is without a doubt the worst possible thing most people can do to their bodies, and except in the case of a few rare individuals, it inevitably leads to lung and vascular disease. For many people it leads to various types of cancer. In my life expectancy calculator, smoking takes 15 years off your life. Also, antiaging quackery will certainly take money out of your wallet and lead to no benefits. In the case of some aggressively promoted treatments, such as growth hormone, there is the real possibility that the purported fountain of youth could contribute to your dying sooner and suffering from numerous adverse effects of the drug.

Many people reading this book are, of course, 60 years old or older. As such, with a well-functioning brain, you are already demonstrating significant survival prowess. My guess is that you have a better chance than the average population of going even beyond the mid-to-late

80s! It is never too late to begin the strategies I have mentioned here, and those with friends and family younger than you should pass this information on to them, because you can't be too young to institute these healthy behaviors.

Well, now that you have another 30 or more years ahead of you, you know that you will be able to do the other 59 things mentioned in this book while looking forward to "Seventy Things To Do When You Are Seventy!"

Other resources:

www.livingto100.com (a life expectancy calculator with feedback for what you are doing right and wrong and some guidance)

www.bumc.bu.edu/centenarian (the New England Centenarian Study website)

25

Learn new tricks

An old dog can learn new tricks! Now that you're 60, it's time to jump out of that easy chair — through new hoops!

by Mel Boring

Mel Boring, a children's writer for 37 years, is the former Web editor of the Institute of Children's Literature Web site. In his mid-60s, he decided to write children's books full time. Boring is the author of twelve books, including *Guinea Pig Scientists: Bold Self-Experimenters in Science and Medicine*, cowritten with Leslie Dendy.

When my 30-something son, Jeremy, was 12, he had a yen to ride a unicycle. Every day, I watched him through the window as he pushed off on that one-wheeled cycle, thrashed at its pedals — and fell. He tried and fell, tried and fell, tried and fell. I was relieved that he was landing on about two inches of Santa Barbara sand — not fail-safe, but he was safe.

After Jeremy had tried for about four hours every day for five days, I looked out and saw him riding the unicycle — all over our bumpy yard. Soon he came crashing through the front door — not on his unicycle, thankfully — shouting that he had learned to ride!

I never learned to ride that unicycle, myself. And after Jeremy left to become "Jeremy Davies," the film actor (*Nell, Going All the Way, Saving Private Ryan*), that unicycle sat in the corner of our garage, unridden. Was it deriding me, I wondered.

That was 17 years ago, and I've tried and fallen, tried and fallen, tried and fallen — and never learned to ride that thing! But I will, by dog! Because I have come to believe what John Rooney says: "The quickest way to become an old dog is to stop learning new tricks."

So here are 60 new tricks I have vowed to learn before the end of my 60s. Won't you join me? You're welcome to try on any of mine for size, or find others that suit you better.

1. Ride that #%(!@$ unicycle!
2. Take ten pounds off my five-foot-six-inch self, and keep it off.
3. Take greater charge of my own health, eating right, exercising regularly — and no more colonoscopies, unless there are signs telling me I really need one!
4. Do my yoga exercises every weekday, taking about half an hour.
5. Ride my Schwinn Airdyne 20 minutes every Monday, Wednesday, and Friday.

6. Ride my recumbent bike with two wheels outside, for 500+ miles a year.
7. Walk our Scottie dog Mac — and me — outdoors, once a week.
8. Drink eight glasses of water every day.
9. Eat more chocolate — dark chocolate — because it's good for my heart!
10. Clear the past three years' clutter off my desk — and keep it clear.
11. Stop being such a "neat freak" sometimes.
12. Learn how to play bridge . . . again — having not played in 40 years!
13. Learn, really learn, to play my banjo, which I've just "picked on" for years.
14. Listen more to one kind of music I haven't yet learned to appreciate: jazz.
15. Go to Alaska, the only one of the 50 states I've never visited.
16. Ride the train across Canada in autumn to see its spectacular beauty.
17. Learn to speak Spanish fluently so that I can talk with most Hispanics.
18. Visit Spain, where a friend has invited us to come and stay for a while.
19. Live the purpose I once preached: to Glorify God and enjoy Him forever.

20. Read the Bible again.
21. Read the Torah.
22. Read the Koran.
23. Read the Book of Mormon.
24. Read one adult book for every five children's books.
25. Learn to illustrate, so I can write and illustrate children's books.
26. Write, illustrate, and sell one picture book.
27. Give more back to writers who ask me for my help.
28. Case-by-case, accept each adversity as part of my life.
29. Stop all fears I can recognize, such as my fear of criticism.
30. Trust others more than I have, because they can see what I won't.
31. Appreciate more, such as what my wife and children say and do for me.
32. Spend more time thinking than watching TV.
33. Do more listening than talking to every person I encounter.
34. Actively change something about me that other people and I don't like — interrupting?
35. Keep some unkept promises, such as helping a friend with lupus write her story.
36. Be more vulnerable (not superior) to people around me than I'd like to think I am.
37. Be more honest and speak more honestly — trusting honesty as the best policy.

38. Allow myself to make some mistakes!

39. Understand one thing a month that I don't right now — such as people who pierce body parts.

40. Make one new friend a month, and spend more time with my best friend.

41. Finish one unfinished book project for each year through age 70.

42. With my wife, have one get-together a month with friends.

43. Phone or e-mail each of my two brothers once a week.

44. Visit my parents' grave site in Milan, Michigan, once before I'm 70.

45. Help my cousin Ray find out where his own mother's grave is.

46. Visit our granddaughter (Ginger) in California, once each year.

47. Say the three most important words to my wife every day, "I love you."

48. Say "I love you" to each of our children, every time I e-mail, write, or see them.

49. Take my wife out for a tasty meal and a good movie (at least) once a month.

50. Do something at least slightly special for my wife's parents twice each year.

51. Thank someone for something they've done for me or given me, once a week.

52. Stop my useless talking back to radio and TV commercials.

53. Write to one company a year to express my appreciation for a helpful product.

54. Take empty cans and bottles to the redemption center instead of the dump.

55. Start calling the "dump" by its proper name, the "sanitary landfill."

56. Try to earn the name "Environmental Wacko" from the opposition — for remembering our environment and doing things to preserve it.

57. Strive to pick myself up after a fall-down failure in no longer than a week.

58. Do some unexpected kindness every day, unexpected by the recipient or me.

59. Throw a party at age 70 with the theme: "What I will do in my next 30 years?"

60. Visit Orcas Island — an easy trick because we're going there next week!

I've put my promises in writing because having you know I've made them will help me keep them. In the half of my 60s still remaining, the 60 tricks will have to be done about one a month — some in a shorter time, others longer. If I'm fortunate enough to get to meet you during the next five years, please ask me how I'm doing on my 60 tricks. Because this advice is as much (or more) for me as it is for you.

Now, when I reach my 70s, maybe I'll ride that #%(!@$ unicycle to Alaska!

Rejuvenate your mind

The more you bombard your brain with new experiences, the more episodic memories you'll create. Stimulating your hippocampus will ensure that the next three decades don't just race by in the blink of an eye!

by Roger K. Pitman, M.D.

Roger K. Pitman, M.D., is a professor of psychiatry at Harvard Medical School. For the past 25 years, he has been conducting internationally recognized research into post-traumatic stress disorder (PTSD) and memory disturbance, working with Vietnam veterans. Dr. Pitman, who lives in West Newbury, Massachusetts, with his wife, Charlotte, and two children, enjoys skiing and sculling.

When I was six or seven, I remember listening to a radio broadcast of the New Year's Eve celebration in Times Square. I had a vague recollection of hearing the same thing the previous year, but it seemed like it was eons ago. Back then, it seemed to take forever for one year to pass.

Recently when I viewed the New Year's Eve festivities in Times Square on TV, it seemed that the same ball that had dropped to announce 2017 had just continued dropping for a few more seconds to announce 2018. The year had passed in the blink of an eye! At the same time, the older I become, the more the reality sinks in that most of my New Years are in the past. The tragic fact of human nature is: "You don't know what you've got 'til it's gone," or at least until it's almost gone. This realization of life's finiteness makes the years that remain seem all the more precious to those in their 60s.

So here is a terrible irony. The older one gets, the more precious the years become; but the older one gets, the more quickly they seem to pass! Is there any remedy to this cruel dilemma? Perhaps so. Have you ever noticed that it seems like it took longer to travel to a new destination than it took to come back, even though the actual time elapsed is the same in each direction? This is another demonstration of the difference between objective and subjective time. The explanation may lie in the phenomenon of novelty. On the way to a new destination, you see things for the first time, but on the way back, you've seen them already. Subjective time may be proportional to novelty; the greater the novelty, the slower time passes. To a young child, almost everything in life is novel, and it just dawdles along. To an adult, life may become just the "same old, same old," and speed by.

Indeed, our brains appear to have a built-in novelty detector in a structure called the hippocampus. The hippocampus, assisted by the frontal lobes, is also critically involved in what is called episodic memory, which is essential to the uniquely human ability to place one's autobiographical life events in a temporal sequence, and thereby experience subjective time. The neuropsychologist Endel Tulving wrote that episodic memory "makes possible mental time travel through subjective time, from the present to the past, thus allowing one to re-experience . . . one's own previous experiences." For us older folks, the episodic memories we already have represent our strong suit, because we have more of them. In contrast, our ability to form new episodic memories decreases as the brain ages, making it imperative that we keep making them, as long as we're able.

What if we in our 60s aren't satisfied with enjoying our memories of the past, but also want time to slow down a bit, so that we can enjoy more of what's left of life in the future? What can we do, short of surgically stimulating our own hippocampi? Apparently, we can stimulate our hippocampi by doing new things. The more new things we do, and the more life episodes we create, the greater becomes our episodic memory, and the longer our sense of time stretches out.

It once was believed that no new neurons (nerve cells) were created in the brain after fetal development; you had all the neurons you were ever going to get at birth, and after that, the number could only go down. A dismal scenario! Recently, however, neuroscience has discovered that new neurons are created in the hippocampus throughout life, a phenomenon called "neurogenesis." Interestingly, evidence exists that exposure to novel experiences stimulates neurogenesis (i.e., creates new nerve cells in the brain). It also promotes the growth of the connections between nerve cells, called "synapses." So, doing new things may do for the brain what physical exercise does for the body.

The more new things we do, or the more we do old things in a new way, the more we can stretch out the life we still have ahead of us. Perhaps this is one reason why older people love to travel. Experiencing new places and people, by definition, adds novelty, and this enriches not only life's content, but also extends its subjective duration. Conversely, if the promoter of a subjectively long life is novelty, then its enemy must be "neophobia" — fear of the new.

Neuropsychology appears to offer those after 60 the following take-home message: If you want to stay young, get out of that rut and do something new! In my case, shortly before my 50th birthday, I took up scuba diving; shortly before my 60th birthday, I took up sculling. When I do these sports, time stands still, and I feel like a kid again! A few months ago, I bought a Cajun accordion. Unfortunately, I haven't had any time to learn how to play it, yet. I wonder how many new neurons that's costing me! The new things that you decide to experience may vary, depending upon where your heart and your interests lead you. Be bold. Be creative. Have fun!

27

Live like a kid

Approach life in your 60s with a child-like curiosity — growing up is a never-ending process!

by Frank J. Miele

Frank J. Miele owns Frank J. Miele Gallery (of contemporary American folk art) in New York. Mr. Miele has lectured on folk art at the American Folk Art Museum in New York, the de Young Museum in San Francisco, and the Amon Carter Museum in Fort Worth, Texas, and writes for art publications.

Now is the time to plan for what you want to do next. I have managed to fill my life with interesting things to do. And I am going to continue to do so.

For 23 years, I practiced law. During this time, I lived on a farm and raised sheep. I even won a blue ribbon at the 4-H Fair one year (well, in truth, I didn't win the ribbon, my ram did!). In January 1987, I was a senior partner in Riker, Danzig, Scherer, Hyland & Perretti, a prestigious New Jersey law firm, when I left to start Hirschl & Adler Folk, a gallery of 18th and 19th century American folk art.

The change in career seemed unusual only to those who did not know me well. My love of art is lifelong. I started to paint as a child and continued painting all through my school years, until I became a junior associate at a large law firm and no longer had the time. Instead, I began to frequent museums and art galleries and, in the process, began to look at art, learn about art, collect art, and eventually, write freelance articles for art magazines. In the process, of course, I unwittingly formed the foundation for a second career.

Why change careers, you might ask, if one has achieved a modicum of success as a lawyer? Why leave the security of one's position to do something so totally different?

At the time, I did not know the answer to that question and did not even think about it. But I know now. I became a lawyer for the sake of my mom and dad. I became an art dealer for me.

My parents — Italian immigrants — never pressured me into any career choice, but I knew, down deep, that I had to become a doctor or a lawyer for them to feel that they had succeeded as parents. That's just the way it was for immigrant parents at the time of my childhood.

It really didn't matter that there were other things that I might have done. Golf and baseball, for example. In high school, my coaches in both sports urged me repeatedly to consider pursuing professional golf or baseball as a career. How could I have ever told my parents that I intended to play golf, or baseball, as a career? I couldn't have.

Since medicine did not interest me, I became a lawyer. Mind you, I have no regrets; I loved the practice of law. Upon reflection, though, I now know that I did so to please my parents. And when I decided to pursue my passion for art, I now know that I did so to please myself.

When I first began to collect art, I was drawn to the work of abstract expressionists. Then I discovered American folk art, an art form that combined my love for American history with my fondness for abstract art. I was smitten. The hard-edged, exaggerated forms of the 18th and 19th century itinerant artists had the same appeal for me as the work of the abstract expressionists, and I consequently changed the focus of my collecting to American folk art.

Hirschl & Adler Folk, therefore, provided the perfect transition from law into art. I remained director there until I discovered the wonderful work being done by contemporary American folk artists. I left in 1991 to start a gallery of my own — the Frank J. Miele Gallery, devoted to the work of these artists.

Beginning with my change in careers, I began to lecture at art museums around the country and write free-lance articles for art magazines, including *The Magazine Antiques, Elle Décor,* and *Art & Antiques.*

Life is filled with so many opportunities to do so many wonderful things. And I have always wanted to do them all. I have a childlike curiosity about life and an insatiable appetite for learning about and doing new things.

I have always believed that you should pursue your passions. Whatever your interests or abilities, you should develop them to the fullest.

I think there is always room in my cup to fill it a bit more. And it is probably that approach to life that has led me, in recent years, to pursue my interest in opera and ballet, onstage.

For the past several years, I have been a supernumerary (I think of "supers" as living props) with the Metropolitan Opera and American Ballet Theatre (ABT). (Inspired by all of the wonderful dancers with whom I appeared onstage, two years ago, I even took ballet classes!) At the Met, I have appeared in *Aida* (as a triumphant warrior), *Turandot* (as a bearer of a sun banner), and in

Don Carlos (as a doctor and as a lawyer—boy, would my parents have been happy!). With ABT, I have appeared in *Swan Lake* (escorting a beautiful lady to the throne of the queen), *La Bayadere* (as a priest), and *Romeo and Juliet* (as an elegant gentleman in the market scene and the ballroom scene). I have also appeared as a super with the Kirov Ballet (*Swan Lake*) and the Birmingham Royal Ballet (*The Two Pigeons*).

I came to classical music and dance late in life because, as a child of a lower middle-class family, I had no exposure to either while growing up. Just reflect upon how society tends to think about growing up. A thing of the past. Something we did as kids. Something behind us. Done. We become "grown-ups" — past tense — at some point in our lives.

That is certainly not my view of things, though. I was asked recently where I grew up. "Past tense?" I asked, in response to the question. "I was growing up in New Jersey earlier in my life," I replied, "and I am now growing up in New York."

"Growing up," I think, should be a never-ending process. It should start when you are born. And stop only when you die.

When friends tell me that they want to retire, I am always horrified. Retire? Retire from what? Life? Living?

Buy a condo in Florida and a studio in New York and then do nothing but sit around and wait to die?

Not for me. When my day of reckoning finally arrives, I can just see myself putting up a fight and arguing with God: "What, leave now? When there is so much more I want to do? No, no, no."

So, now, at the (biological) age of 66, am I planning to sit back and to do nothing?

No, not me. I'll plan, instead, for what I want to do next.

Get rich quick

Harness your entrepreneurial spirit and drive it forward in a sixth-decade business. You can have a millionaire retirement!

by Loral Langemeier

Loral Langemeier, a successful business and motivational speaker, is the author of *The Millionaire Maker*, which outlines her concept of the wealth cycle process, a step-by-step plan for building wealth. Committed to helping people create unimaginable success, she is also the founder of a financial education company, Live Out Loud (www.liveoutloud.com).

Growing up in the Eisenhower 1950s with parents who endured the deprivations of the Great Depression and war shortages, we learned to operate as follows: Make money, spend money. We were the ultimate consumers — the TV Generation. In actuality, this is not the way to do it. You shouldn't buy a lifestyle, no matter how many Ralph Lauren ads catch your eye. You should buy cash flow, producing assets, and then get a lifestyle. That's the better sequence.

Two of my clients, both in their late 50s, from Cincinnati, Ohio, had the "make money, spend money" equation down pat. They were psychologically invested in looking pretty, which kept them poor. They weren't thinking long-term. Paying yourself first is an axiom of the wealthy — invest a portion of your money instead of spending it all. The concept of paying yourself first is about creating wealth to run circles around your debt, so that you can spiral up your wealth and easily pay off your debt. Those who do not understand, or misunderstand, this concept often live in a mindset of fear — the exact scarcity thinking that traps you. Your cash flow will pay off your debt. Pay yourself first, build the account, and amass what you need to invest.

My powerful, encouraging vision and advice for all wartime babies is this: A millionaire retirement is more than possible in your 60s. With this way of dealing with money and finances, the only thing that's passive is your income.

Entrepreneurship is the single biggest source of wealth in this country. By establishing your own business, you can increase and keep more of your cash. It takes a huge commitment mentally, physically, and spiritually, and if you've feared starting your own business, it's understandable. If you conquer your fear, however, you'll find out just how available success is.

I coach families to establish "wealth cycles" — where your assets are producing other assets and cash flow — by starting a business that maximizes your current skill set. Your wealth cycle propels you to start your dream business, whether it is a floral shop, a nursery, or a bed-and-breakfast inn. Maybe you have an idea for a new product or want to establish a charitable organization. Get into action now to plan the short-term strategies that will help you learn to earn.

Tycoons have mastered the skill of creating companies to support their visions. Your number one task is to refocus your skills past the hobby stage and put in the time, energy and resources to direct them into a viable business. With your skill set, you will create a cash machine, bringing in extra money to invest — to get yourself out of debt, avoid bankruptcy, and support your extended family financial plans (such as sending kids to college).

While learning to create this cash machine, you also are learning how to start and manage a business. Like most people, you may have invested time, education, and training in a profession, perhaps putting off making good money until later in life. The time is now. Even if you are debt-ridden from chasing those big career breaks and living a lifestyle beyond your means, you can apply these skills to any future dream business.

In order to learn to earn and keep those earnings, I require my clients to create an entity — a corporation, partnership, or limited liability company (LLC) that supports a viable business strategy based on each client's existing skill set. Then, real money can be made and experience can be gained in running a business.

Entities protect your personal assets, enabling you to take advantage of hundreds, if not thousands of dollars in tax savings — even retroactively. Your personal holdings should stay at a minimum and your business should be structured to prevent legal losses, ranging from lawsuits to IRS audits and insurance claims. Hold on to more of your hard-earned money inside a corporate structure, taking full advantage of the highest tax savings allowed by law. By setting up your life as a business, you start thinking like a business — a profitable and productive entity.

The initial cost for setting up each of these entities is usually around $600, which will be more than covered by the revenue you retain each year. The entities should include a relationship with knowledgeable professionals who have the entrepreneurial mindset and skills to maximize how to keep more of what you make, using tax strategies for the wealthy. This is your team — a community of wealthy people with vision and passions like your own. They are your bridge from doing what you have to do to make money, to doing what you really love to do. And, in the process, they will let your assets and businesses make money for you.

Though I have made more money than I ever thought possible in my life, I've also made many mistakes along the way. I've made bad investments and bad choices, and I've lost money. Most wealthy people have, and it's your team that reminds you that it's part of the learning curve. Ultimately, I've made good investments and good choices, and have never made the same mistake twice. My team has taught me to give myself permission to fail. I began to live outside of my comfort zone, which expands daily.

One of my mentors once told me that when my annual income becomes my monthly income, I'd just be getting started with wealth building. That seemed unbelievable to me. Now, there are times when I make that kind of money in a single day.

Don't wait until you've accumulated a lot of cash or have identified a particular investment to build wealth — that's the biggest mistake people make. In today's markets, people without much background knowledge are investing in real estate and doubling their money. Invest some time in learning and you'll really be able to turn your situation around. Instead of babysitting nonperforming assets, you actually could be nurturing some real growth and income.

Don't go on a debt diet. Restricting and limiting your thinking will absolutely destroy your opportunity to grow truly wealthy. I don't take debt issues lightly; what I propose is that you take a positive approach to your finances and don't put getting out of debt as your first priority. What you need to do, instead, is direct your energy to building your vision and following your wealth plan.

As you begin to learn more about the wealth cycle process, you will switch from retail-therapy addiction to what I call asset addiction. Nothing conditions the brain to invest like a nice, steady return on investments.

Ready? Get set, and then *go!*

29

Start a business

Work after 60? Think "start-up," not "wind-down!" Life is too short not to be mentally engaged. Do what you love — on your own terms!

by Virgil Scudder

Virgil Scudder is president of Virgil Scudder & Associates, an international media- training and communications-consulting firm based in New York, which he started with his son when he was 54. His clients include CEOs of many Fortune 500 companies and leaders of business and government in Europe, Asia, Australia, and North America. Mr. Scudder entered the media-training field after a successful stint as a public-relations executive and an award-winning career as a broadcast journalist at ABC News, WINS, and NBC in New York.

A lot of things have changed by the time you hit 60. You are no longer the terror of the tennis courts (if you ever were). Your hair is gray — or would be if you didn't put chemicals on it — and there's probably less of it. More people call you "sir," or "madam." Depending on your employer, you're probably retired, or facing retirement fairly soon. Or maybe you've already been pushed out.

This is a great time to start a business.

Why would you want to? It's quite simple. Owning your own business enables you to manage your life better. You can decide when to go visit the grandchildren, or when to take a day off to play golf. Yes, you'll probably work long hours. You can decide, however, what those hours are. Most important of all, you can decide when — or whether — to retire.

You've got a lot of advantages at 60 that you didn't have when you were young. You probably have a little money socked away — good; you're going to need it to start a business. Most of your family obligations, such as college, are probably well behind you. You're in a better position to take a chance.

You have a lot of experience. You're not going to make many of the mistakes that younger people make. You have loads of contacts — a much wider social circle than you did at 20; those contacts can be valuable to you. You likely have a credit rating established, so you'll be able to borrow start-up money.

Most important of all, you have your brain. While your body has been slowing down over the years, your mind has been growing. You may not be able to remember names or facts as well as you once did, but your ability to reason and "problem solve" has never been greater.

When many of my colleagues were talking retirement, I was thinking about new directions. So, I gave up a good job as senior vice president of the world's largest public relations firm to set up my own shop. Why? I thought I could do even better on my own.

Wasn't this move a big risk? Of course it was. Sometimes the biggest risk is not to take a risk at all.

I invited a colleague to join me in my new venture. He decided that it entailed too much risk, and said he preferred the security of a big company over a tiny start-up. A few months later, he was let go. Had he joined me, we'd probably still be business partners today.

Here's a key thing to remember: You don't have to start another General Motors to be successful. It's fine to start a little business that makes you happy. Profitability and job satisfaction are more important than size.

When my son, Ken, and I established Virgil Scudder & Associates, a media-training firm based in New York, our goal was threefold: to be small, to be the best in our field, and to be profitable. The game plan worked. Today, we coach and counsel CEOs of some of the world's biggest Fortune 500 companies. And, we've been profitable from day one.

How do you decide what business to be in? Look at what you're good at and what you like. Where possible, pursue your interests and passions.

A friend of mine who grew up loving cowboy movies is now a leading provider of authentic cowboy paraphernalia — guns, saddles, horses, and even the experienced horsemen to ride them — to the TV and movie studios in Los Angeles. One of my neighbors in New Jersey left a good corporate job to buy and run an Italian restaurant (he's English); by the way, it's doing very well. A retired friend of mine in California decided to get rid of a few trinkets around the house, so she put them up for sale on eBay. When they quickly sold at a favorable price, she was hooked. Now, she has a small business buying and selling collectibles on eBay, and she loves it.

Once you've decided what kind of business to start, define your value proposition. Why should someone come to you, instead of a competitor? Is it price? Quality? Service? What do you want people to think of when they think about your business?

Build your network of suppliers and advisers right away. You'll need a good lawyer and an accountant, for starters.

Start small, unless you have a lot of cash, or your plans require a lot of cash. If you can begin on a part-time basis while keeping your day job, better still.

Draw up a budget. Don't risk more than you can afford to lose. Identify your start-up costs, your overhead, and your operating expenses. Don't overpay yourself.

Publicize your business through advertising, networking, and public appearances. Put out a newsletter with tips that your customers and prospects can use. Ours goes to over 800 people — executives of large corporations, clients, and prospective clients. It gives them tips on effective public speaking, how to handle a crisis, and how to handle the news media. There is no hard sell. As a result, it gets read and it brings us business.

Join a business-development network — or start one. We're members of one in New York that has brought us many thousands of dollars in business, but had the unexpected benefit of connecting us with some great and reliable suppliers. They have literally saved us tens of thousands of dollars through their expertise.

Put up a good Web site. Make it easy to read, easy to navigate, and keep it updated. A Web site that has dated information sends a message that yours is a careless, sloppy business.

Most important, keep your business fresh by periodically examining it — to be sure you're up-to-date and ahead of competitors.

Finally, think about the future. Do plan to sell your enterprise, pass it along to a family member or colleague, franchise it, or just shut it down when you retire? It's time to make those decisions now, so you control the outcome.

As you hit the later decades of your working life, ask yourself a question: Do you really want to spend the rest of your life on the beach? Or would you prefer the adventure of having your own business? For me, it was an easy call.

30

Make a commitment

At 60, you have skills that are desired by volunteer organizations everywhere. Share them by joining the Peace Corps!

by Laura Schatzberg

Adventurous from an early age, Laura Schatzberg moved from New York to Israel in her late teens. For the next decade she lived on a kibbutz, served in the Israeli Army, and completed a B.A. at the Hebrew University of Jerusalem. She lives in California. Ms. Schatzberg has studied photography, computers, and natural history. She has written essays for local publications, and has taught English as a second language. Teaching is her first love, and she plans to continue in that field.

Every few years I need to shake myself up, do something different to give me a new perspective. I'm still me, but I like to look at life from a different angle. As my life shifts, I remember things that I may have thought of doing at one time but then forgot. Joining the Peace Corps was one of those things.

When I was 13, the idea of service was planted in my mind. Thirty-nine years later, that seed of service germinated. Most people who join the Peace Corps are between the ages of 20–30, but there's no upper age limit, and the corps welcomes late bloomers (like myself) as well as those who were otherwise occupied when they were younger.

Serving in the Peace Corps is a significant commitment at any age. You sign on for two years, and each assignment has its particular challenges. I was glad I could summon skills from my varied previous experiences to assist me in meeting those challenges. My years of living independently made the isolation easier to bear. Having lived without electricity for many years meant that the power and water outages did not feel like deprivation. Having lived and traveled abroad prepared me for different cultures.

My previous experiences abroad also taught me that sensitivity and observation are necessary to maintain cultural appropriateness, but also that people are people wherever you are. As an older woman (and in Namibia, where I served, life expectancy is in the early 40s), I was often called *ouma* 'grandmother,' and I did not need to navigate the minefield of macho aggression. As an outsider, I could perceive that disturbing phenomenon with the younger women who were its target. But ultimately, people want the same thing everywhere: to be treated well and acknowledged as individuals.

Volunteers are sent to countries that request assistance. Namibia is a newly independent country that has chosen English as its official language, and because I had had some experience and training in teaching ESL, I was given the assignment of teaching the Namibians. The goal of my service was first to teach them English and also to leave them better equipped to teach English on their own. One of the daily challenges of my work with the Peace Corps was that it was not obvious to me that I was accomplishing this goal. Toward the end of my time there I received some feedback to indicate that I had contributed to my school's level of English and had encouraged a culture of reading. I hope I did.

But I was also a main benefactor of my service. I believe I vastly improved my interpersonal, communications skills. I used to be a very reluctant public speaker, but standing in front of five classes a day made me much less shy. Eventually, speaking in front of the entire school or a leadership camp of 80 children became just another task to be performed. I frequently needed to work as part of a team, both in school and with other Peace Corps volunteers, and in the process, I strengthened my listening abilities. Before, I had always been a grudge holder, but working with children, who can insult you one minute and hug you the next, cured me of that. I found that if I became angry, I was able to get over it quickly and go on with the lesson. I found that I could impart stern discipline when necessary in school and be relaxed and approachable outside of school.

My learning curve was constant and steep. Due to the fact that human resources in certain fields are spread thin, someone who knows a little becomes an expert. Since I am comfortable with computers, I became an "expert," performing computer functions I had never used for various school tasks and learning how to teach basic computing.

Probably most importantly, I learned from children who had experienced terrible, sad events that life goes on. It is crucial not to dwell on losses but to find humor and joy in what you are doing now. Having a position of responsibility for children made me an adult. Earlier in my life, I had avoided that designation, with the stodginess and boredom it had implied to me. What being an adult means to me now is the ability to handle situations that may or may not be to my liking and to be part of a collaborative process that produces results acceptable to all involved.

Stretching my skills and challenging the limits of my comfort zone made my Peace Corps experience one of the best things I've done in my life. My desire to learn about and experience other cultures and be where I felt needed inspired me to join. If you feel so inspired, but a two-year commitment seems undoable, seek out opportunities that suit your situation — many other organizations arrange volunteer opportunities abroad for much shorter periods. Or look for ways to volunteer right in your own neighborhood. Giving back, whether halfway around the world or in your own backyard, is very enriching.

31

Discover what matters

A life-threatening diagnosis doesn't have to mean that life is over. Sometimes it means that life needs a new focus.

by Judith E. Glaser

Judith E. Glaser is an American author, academic, business executive and organizational anthropologist. She is the founder and chief executive officer of Benchmark Communications, Inc., an executive coaching and management consulting company based in Boston. Glaser is also the co-founder and chairman of the Creating WE Institute. During her career, she has worked with clients including Clairol, Citibank, Pfizer, Burberry, American Airlines, and Verizon.

Glaser has authored seven books including best-seller *Creating WE: Change I-Thinking to We-Thinking & Build a Healthy Thriving Organization.*

On the morning of September 11, 2001, while the world was watching in horror as the World Trade Center came tumbling down, my doctor uttered four terrible words: "You have breast cancer." My cancer was small but very aggressive; doctors also found cancer in my bone marrow.

My doctor held my hand and told me I'd be okay, but I felt only terror. At 55, I was afraid my life was over. My mother, after all, had died of cancer. Memories of my mother's suffering swirled through my head. She discovered a melanoma on her leg when I was 12. I had to force myself to remember that our cancers were not alike — and that how we handled them would also be very different.

Mom's cancer arrived in her body 45 years ago, when doctors didn't know as much as they do today about how melanomas spread into the lymph system. It was also a time when cancer was a huge stigma — people wouldn't talk about it — and they wouldn't share their pain and suffering.

Everyone I have spoken with who struggles through cancer experiences a personal and unique transformation. For me, breast cancer brought me down to my own ground zero.

I was scheduled for two operations, the strongest chemo, and radiation. While my mother went underground about her cancer, I chose to reach out to everyone in my life and share — something I had shunned in the past. With each business success, you see, I began to fear failure. Rather than reach out for support as the pressure mounted, I kept my fears inside. I believe the fears turned to rage, which manifested itself as cancer.

Now, I felt the need to connect with everyone about what mattered most — to stay in conversations about health, to be about giving without fear of losing, and to get my focus off my condition. I woke up every morning asking myself what my life was going to be all about, because I knew I could not continue with the stressful lifestyle I had created. Life needed to be more than just work.

As you turn 60, when life hands you a challenge to meet — a frightening diagnosis, a heart-breaking event — see it as an opportunity to discover what matters most, and learn how to live again.

My process of learning to live again began when, out of the blue, Nancy Hunt, an old friend, called me looking for a phone number. We talked about our lives. I shared my story, she shared hers. We decided to meet for coffee, and it was then that Nancy told me a story that gave my life new meaning.

From Nancy I learned that on 9-11 her significant other, Nile Rodgers, lost a close friend on American Airlines flight #11. Within a week, Nile arranged for 100 actors, musicians, and street people affected by 9-11 to rerecord *We Are Family*, the famous '70s song that Nile wrote for Sister Sledge with his late partner Bernard Edwards. The retaping turned into a documentary built around the recording sessions and directed by Spike Lee. The film touched many lives. And Nancy and Nile decided to create the We Are Family Foundation. As I completed my chemo, I became their vice president.

Today, We Are Family Foundation is doing great work in the world. We're building schools in Africa, for example, and sending students as U.S. ambassadors to be part of the new beginnings. We are also creating programs for schoolchildren to learn about tolerance and peace. We Are Family Foundation enabled me to see the world with new eyes. It reminded me that what's most important about life is living with passion.

In the four years since my cancer scare, passion, healing, and rebirth have become the central themes in my life. I've found wonderful women to partner with to birth exciting projects focused on health and healing. With Mary Wang, president of DKNY, and 25 other women executives, for example, we formed WITHH (Women in Transition Helping and Healing), to support women who lost their spouses and children in 9-11. Today the foundation supports a New York City school with educational programs so students can better their lives.

I've also become a best-selling author. My book *Creating We: Change I-Thinking to We-Thinking & Build a Healthy Thriving Organization* made the Amazon business book best-seller list, was chosen by *Forbes* in 2005 as a business book to read, and *Business Book Review* chose it as one of the best books of 2005.

I give all the credit to my bout with cancer. Ironically, cancer helped "remind me" how to be healthy. It refocused my attention on living life fully and loving more deeply. Cancer has given me the platform to tell the story of relationships — and the power they have to heal and help the world grow stronger. *Creating We* focuses on creating power with others and coaches leaders to embrace an engaging style of leadership.

Lastly, based on my husband Rich's research on a cancer cure that instructs cancer cells on how to return to normal, I came up with a concept called Vital Instincts. Basically, we all have the instinct to bond and connect with others. When those connections break, however, we retreat into an I-centric world. But we live in a We-centric world, so we must be willing to reach out to others and accept their help to get through our darkest hours. My husband's work inspired three principles for health that I live by every day:

I will allow others to be there for me.
I will share my feelings. I'm not allowed to fake it!
I will view the world as a positive place.
The cup is half full, not half empty.

My family has become my rock and salvation. Rich has helped me to redefine what love is all about. And I treasure the deep relationship that I have developed with my daughter. A few weeks into my treatment she said, "Mom, I wouldn't wish cancer on anyone, ever, but I must tell you that since you've been diagnosed, we talk more on the phone, we see each other more, and I love having you around this way. I hope this will continue. I just love what our relationship is becoming."

Life moves in strange ways. As I turn 60, I am glad to be alive. I feel blessed to have discovered what matters most. New beginnings can rise, indeed, from seemingly unbeatable odds.

Section Five

MONEY (THAT'S WHAT I WANT)

(Barrett Strong, 1960;
The Beatles, 1964)

32

Milk your cash cow

When you retire, your 401(k) plan should be working for you, not your company. It's time to turn your retirement plan into an income-generating machine!

by Jeff Harris, Ch.F.C.

Jeff Harris, Ch.F.C., is a financial adviser, consultant, and the author of *Retire Rich and Happy: 12 Secrets to Retirement Success.*

Let's face it. Retirement plans like 401(k)s and other pension/profit-sharing plans are great vehicles for building nest eggs. And if you have one, count yourself fortunate. With both plans, you can deduct contributions from your taxable income and gain tax-deferred growth of earnings, as well.

You've reached the magic age of 60 — right on the doorstep of your golden years. You've changed, and your needs are changing. You'll want your retirement plan to become an ongoing income stream, so that you'll have the money to do what you want, when you want.

Unfortunately, the investment choices inside your 401(k) are not the options you'll need to fund the retirement lifestyle you want to have. That's because retirement plans are primarily designed to attract and retain employees. And in many ways, they're geared more toward the needs of the company than those of the retirees. Your former employer will never tell you this, but allowing retirees to stay in these plans is viewed as a "necessary evil." Why?

1) *Once you retire, you become a drain on your company's resources.* You're no longer contributing to the bottom line; you're taking away from it. Company plans aren't designed to be very friendly to retirees — your family will be forced to take the money from the plan within five years of your passing.

Being forced to take out big chunks from your plan could cause big income tax bills for your heirs. Still, if your company plan requires them to take the money out, they won't have a choice.

2) *Fiduciary responsibility limits investment choices.* Congress requires business owners and officers to make sure their retirement plans are run for the benefit of the employees. This means that they have a legal obligation to select prudent investment choices for the retirement plan.

Owners and officers could be subject to unlimited personal liability if they don't fulfill their fiduciary obligations as required by ERISA (the Employees Retirement Income Security Act). That's why most plans limit the number of investment choices they offer to no more than 10–15. Fewer investment options mean fewer potential "problems" for owners and officers.

3) *You needed growth while you were working, but now you need income.* If you look carefully, you'll find that most of the investment choices in retirement plans are growth-oriented. They're chosen because that's what employees want. Little thought is given to preserving and protecting principal, because you're adding money regularly to your plan.

Once you retire, however, everything changes. You're no longer putting money into your plan; now you're taking it out. And if you're still using growth-oriented investments like mutual funds, which follow an index such as the Standard & Poor's 500 (the 500 largest companies in the United States), when you need income, you could get hurt badly — really badly.

The "income-generating secret"

Depending on where you are in your 60s, you are either in the planning stages or already retired. There is a simple key to generating an attractive retirement income while striving to preserve and protect your nest egg. But here's where the Catch-22 setup comes in: To use your retirement plan as retirement income, you must have investment choices that aren't in most 401(k) plans.

This is why you should create a portfolio that generates the income you need to live on from dividends and interest alone. Here's what you must do: Roll over your 401(k) to your own self-directed IRA — to enjoy a whole new world of investment options that includes everything you'll need to convert your retirement plan into an amazing cash cow. Remember, you can roll over your 401(k), and almost any other retirement plan, to your own IRA — tax free.

Now you're ready to build that income portfolio. You'll need a combination of preferred and common stocks that pay high dividends, some real estate investment trusts (REITS), government and corporate bonds, and maybe some FDIC-insured bank CDs.

Ideally, all the money you'll need to live comfortably will come from the income these holdings generate. You won't have to worry about stock market ups and downs, because the "moolah" will keep flowing, regardless of what the stock market does — or does not — do.

A case in point

Back in the late 1990s, stocks were setting all-time records. It seemed as if stocks just kept going up.

Suppose you retired in July 1999 with $750,000 in your 401(k) and left the money invested in mutual funds that followed the Standard & Poor's 500 index.

You felt very comfortable taking out 6 percent, or $45,000, per year to live on, because the Standard & Poor's 500 index had averaged more than 15 percent annually over the past 20 years. At this rate, you could easily increase your withdrawals over time, as your money grew. But in March 2000, stocks began sinking and continued sliding down, down, down — for three long, heartbreaking years, culminating in the worst meltdown since the Great Depression.

By December 31, 2005, your original nest egg of $750,000 would have dropped to $412,586, for an average annual return of –1.19 percent. Oops! If you had converted your 401(k) into a cash cow, your nest egg would have been worth $825,747 by December 31, 2005, for an average annual return of 7.50 percent. Big difference!

What if you need help?

It's possible that you may need some help in building this portfolio. And since we're talking about your retirement, you don't want to take unnecessary chances. If you make a mistake with a small sum of money, it's not a big deal. If you make the same mistake with a large sum, however, the damage is magnified. You don't have years to make up for losses — as you did when you were working.

If you need help, and your assets are enough to warrant it, look for a registered investment adviser who will work with you on a fee-for-service basis (you don't have to worry about sales commissions). Choose someone with a professional designation, such as a Certified Financial Planner (CFP) or a Chartered Financial Consultant (ChFC); these professionals are required to meet minimum levels of proficiency and attend continuing education programs. Finally, your candidate should have a minimum of ten years of experience working with retirees.

Now that you're getting ready to retire — or even if you've already retired, you should seriously consider rolling over that company 401(k) to your own self-directed IRA. You'll want that cash cow to give you all the "moolah" you'll need to live richly and happily.

33

Budget for 100 years

Extend your savings along with your life span — for a comfortable retirement.

by Anna M. Rappaport, F.S.A., M.A.A.A.

Anna M. Rappaport, F.S.A., M.A.A.A., founded Anna Rappaport Consulting in 2005, after retiring from Mercer Human Resource Consulting. She chairs the Society of Actuaries Committee on Post-Retirement Needs and Risks, which is active in building solutions for a better retirement for Americans. Ms. Rappaport has worked on retirement issues within the American Academy of Actuaries and is on the boards of the National Academy of Social Insurance, the Pension Research Council, the Women's Institute for a Secure Retirement (WISER), and the Actuarial Foundation.

Whether already settled into your retirement or looking forward to it with anticipation, it's not too late to plan for the unexpected at 60. Like many in the Golden Watch Generation, you've anticipated that this new stage of life will open up a whole new world of opportunities — for seeing family and friends, for travel, and for other leisure activities. But you could be fooling yourself. According to recent research conducted by the Society of Actuaries (www.soa.org), there are serious gaps between perceptions about retirement and reality.

Risky assumptions

In fact, when planning for retirement, many people make assumptions that reveal a total lack of understanding that can be dangerous. Actuaries say people are living longer — one spouse will survive to 100 in approximately five to 15 of every 100 couples. This is good news, for certain, but many people plan only with an average life span in mind. This runs counter to the latest statistical evidence that says that of half of the married couples, aged 65 in 2005, both partners are likely to survive to age 80. This means that too few people are considering the probability that they'll live another 15 years, struggling financially in later years because they budgeted only to the average life span. The solution: You've got to consider ways to extend your savings, or find alternate money that can kick in later in life.

Too few couples acknowledge that one partner will outlive the other by a significant period of time — a mistaken belief to be sure, actuaries say. A lot of these surviving partners are going to be women (57 percent of Americans over age 65 are women, 43 percent are men).

It is a trap to plan based on your current situation while failing to focus on the needs of the survivor. Instead, plan as a couple, making sure that the surviving spouse will be well provided for. If pension income is available, use a joint and survivor option. Also consider the possibility of a survivor annuity, life insurance, or a trust to help protect the surviving spouse.

The timing of retirement is not always up to the individual (nearly four in ten people retire before they plan or want to). Many people in their 60s and beyond plan to work in retirement. You may be able to phase into retirement or work part-time. This is certainly an admirable goal; however, it is important not to rely on it solely when planning. Disability, family members in poor health, and unforeseen changes in the labor market and demand can easily make employment opportunities difficult or unrealistic. Statistics reveal that more than six million older Americans are poor, or nearly poor. Almost 30 percent of older unmarried women fall into this category, compared to 8 percent of older married couples. A simple factor we don't always take into consideration is inflation's effect on prices — especially if the money we've got isn't growing as fast.

Filling the gap

How do you keep the good times rolling, when working is not an option? Figure out the guaranteed monthly income (Social Security, pension benefits) that will be received, no matter how long you or your partner live. If your guaranteed, regular monthly income doesn't cover your more realistic, projected, regular living expenses, consider an immediate annuity to provide added income — guaranteed for life. You can buy an annuity to start at any age: immediately on retirement, or later. Alternatively, you can buy longevity insurance — with income to start much later, say at age 85. This will allow you to safely plan to use most of your other assets by age 85, when the longevity insurance starts to provide monthly payments.

Remember, buying an annuity is not right for everyone. A good guide on this topic is "Making Your Money Last for a Lifetime," a booklet from the Women's Institute for a Secure Retirement (WISER) (www.wiser.heinz.org) and the Actuarial Foundation (www.actuarialfoundation.org.).

Assuming that unpleasant and unexpected events (including illness, the premature death of a spouse, or the need for long-term care) will only happen to others is, of course, unwise. In 2004, the cost for a semiprivate room in a nursing home averaged $61,685 per year. The average cost for a home health aide was $18 per hour; if just four hours of care were needed each day, it would add up to $26,000 per year.

Private, long-term care insurance is a good solution for middle-income Americans with savings that could be wiped out; it can help protect the surviving spouse. Without such insurance, savings sometimes are used to care for the first to become ill and die, leaving the survivor with little but Social Security.

For many people, particularly those without pensions, their house is their largest asset and may be their only source of significant savings. Many people want to continue to live in their home and will own it free and clear by the time they retire. They may need added income to live comfortably. Reverse mortgages are an option that allow you to get monthly income based on the value of your home, while you stay in it; the payments can be guaranteed for life.

Many people have already paid off mortgages and don't have much debt at 60. If you're making substantial payments on outstanding debt, pay it off and be sure to think about how it will impact on your finances in retirement.

Eyeing the bottom line

If you don't already have a plan in place by age 60, it's not too late to start. As part of your planning, it is essential to understand the risks and uncertainties during later years, along with corresponding financial products that can be used to insure those risks. With this knowledge, you can then decide which options work for you.

34

Buy and hold

Despite conventional wisdom, a well-diversified portfolio of equities is the only historically sound way to financial security — over the next 30 years. Build a nest egg that will outlive you!

by Nick Murray

Nick Murray has been a financial advisory professional for more than fifty years. He is one of the industry's premier speakers, and the author of twelve books for financial services professionals, the latest of which is *Around the Year with Nick Murray: Daily Readings for Financial Advisors.* His one book for clients, *Simple Wealth, Inevitable Wealth,* has sold nearly a quarter million copies. (www.nickmurray.com).

Conventional wisdom says that as you turn 60 and start preparing for retirement, you cut back on your "growth" investments in equities and build up your "income" portfolio of bonds. As usual, the conventional wisdom is no wisdom at all. And in this instance, it's a prescription for financial disaster, later on. The false premise of investing after 60 is that bonds are "safe" and stocks are "risky." Once you understand what risk and safety really are, you'll see that equities are by far the "safer" choice over the course of your retirement — which, today, can run three decades.

The average retirement age in the United States is always the point at which Social Security retirement benefits become available, which in 2018, is 62. Literally half the people who retire each year do so at this age, and for this reason.

Consider an average retiring couple: a 62-year-old man and his 62-year-old wife. Assume that neither smokes. According to the actuarial tables currently used by America's life insurance companies, what do you suppose is the joint life expectancy of these perfectly average folks? That is, at what age will the second person die?

The answer is 92. And like all actuarial statistics, that's an average. The actuaries are saying that for exactly half of all 62-year-old, nonsmoking couples, at least one spouse will live even longer . . . and will continue to need an income!

Now, think about living costs, and how they rise over long periods of time. Measured by the Consumer Price Index, living costs have gone up an average of 3 percent per year, for the last eight decades or so. At that inflation rate, it will take about $2.45 in the 30th year of retirement to buy what a dollar bought in the first year. This tells you that the real financial risk of a modern, three-decade retirement isn't that you'll lose your money, but that you'll outlive it. Stated another way, the doomsday risk of retirement investing isn't loss of principal, but extinction of purchasing power.

If this seems like an abstraction to you, or if you don't immediately see how erosion of purchasing power becomes the ultimate risk for long-lived retirees, consider the humble, first-class postage stamp. As recently as 1980 (that is, 38 years ago), a stamp cost 15 cents. Early in 2006, it went up to 39 cents. In 2018, it's 50 cents. That's a pretty good proxy for the reality of slow, grinding inflation over the last four decades or so — a period during which inflation was quite subdued.

If the monster risk of long retirements is erosion of purchasing power, wherein is true "safety"? Of course, safety is implicit in those investments which have most reliably preserved — and even enhanced — purchasing power. By this critical definition, stocks don't just provide a higher return than bonds. They're much safer than bonds.

Since the beginning of 1926, consumer prices have inflated at an average annual rate of 3 percent. By the most widely accepted calculation, long-term, high-quality corporate bonds (with interest reinvested) provided an average annual return of just about 6 percent, over the same period.

Large-company common stocks, by the same methodology, compounded at 10.4 percent. And small-company common stocks scored even better: 12.7 percent. This is actually quite staggering, when you think it through: After inflation, or adding 3 percent for inflation to 12.7 percent, stocks netted 15.7 percent, meaning the total real return of equities has been upwards of three times that of bonds. In the long run — and a three-decade retirement is about the longest run you and I have left — stocks have beaten inflation to a pulp.

Ah, yes, say the skeptics, but what about the risk? To which the investor with a 30-year investing time horizon can only reply: What risk?

You see, in the couple of hundred years since Alexander Hamilton started running the Treasury Department, the number of rolling, 30-year periods in which American common stocks have produced a negative return is — you guessed it — zero. (A new, rolling, 30-year period starts every January 1.) Like Mark Twain's death, reports of the long-term risk of owning equities have been greatly exaggerated.

And, for the record, the last 30-year stretch in which the real (net after inflation) return of bonds beat that of stocks ended during the Civil War!

Granted, over shorter time horizons, stocks are much more volatile than bonds. But volatility isn't risk, because time erases its effects. For example, the Standard & Poor's 500 Stock Index has declined an average of 30 percent, 12 times since the end of WWII. (The mildest of these bear markets took the Index down just about 20 percent; the largest, a hair under 50 percent.) That's mighty volatile by anyone's standards.

But during those same 60 years, the Index went from 20 (at this writing) to 1,300 — not even counting dividends. The more you can stay focused on the long-term reality, the less the volatility will bother you.

Yes, you may say, but we need retirement income, and bonds yield more than stocks do. Once again, as we saw with "risk" and "safety," you're falling victim to bad definitions. In this case, you're equating "yield" with "income."

Current yield is only one element of an investment's income-producing potential. The other, of course, is appreciation. Both the yield and the appreciation in your portfolio are available to be taken as income, without invading your capital. And when you measure a portfolio's income-generating capacity by its long-term total return, and not just by its current yield, once again, stocks offer the overwhelming income advantage.

So what, at the end of the day, is the risk of holding equities instead of bonds in a three-decade retirement? Sad to say, it's that you'll one day mistake a plain, garden-variety, average 30 percent market decline for the end of the world, and panic out. Indeed, the long-term risk of holding equities is between your ears.

If you don't lose faith — if you don't panic — history suggests that your money will outlive you . . . instead of the other way around.

35

Use some will power

No more excuses. It's time to put your affairs in order.

by Sanford J. Schlesinger, Esq.

Sanford J. Schlesinger, a founding partner of Schlesinger, Gannon & Lazetera in New York, has written more than 200 articles on estate planning for legal journals and newspapers. A former adjunct professor of law at Columbia Law School, New York Law School, and University of Miami Law School. Mr. Schlesinger is a former chairman of the New York State Bar Association, Trusts and Estates section.

You've heard it time and again: "You need an estate plan." Otherwise, how are you going to divvy up assets so that your heirs avoid inheritance horror stories? Well, no more excuses. You're one of the millions of individuals who will turn 60 this year.

Your retirement years are more likely to be stress-free — and your heirs grateful — if you make sure your money and your property are well-managed now, arrange for their distribution, and plan for the hereafter.

If you've already drawn up an estate plan, you're fortunate. Now is the time for you (or you and your spouse) to sit down and focus on a review, and possible revision, of your estate plan. And, if you haven't established such a plan yet, now is the time.

A step-by-step plan

1. *Consult a professional adviser.* Since a good estate plan deals with complicated gift-tax, estate-tax, and income-tax concepts, you'll first want to select someone you can trust to draw up your plan and prepare documents. Probably that adviser will be an attorney with estate planning as a specialty. Possibly — if you have enough assets — the team should include an accountant, a wealth manager, and/or an insurance adviser.

2. *Prepare a detailed list of assets and liabilities.* Since an estate plan is designed to transmit wealth, your adviser will need to know the nature and extent of your assets. Your second step, then, is to specify if each asset is owned either solely by you or jointly with someone else. If any asset has a beneficiary designation, such as a life insurance policy, pension plan, profit-sharing plan, or IRA, the designated beneficiary for that asset should be named.

3. *Select an executor.* Even people with nominal savings and little property need a will. Should you die without

one, state law — not you — will decide who gets your assets and property. In preparing your will, you first need to select your executor (known as a "personal representative" in some jurisdictions). The executor is responsible for collecting your assets after your death, paying any debts, paying any taxes due from your estate, and distributing the remaining assets to your beneficiaries, in accordance with the terms of your will. You'll need to select one or more trusted individuals to serve as your executor. You may also consider naming a bank or trust company, or a combination of the two.

4. *List your bequests.* Are you of a philanthropic mind? Consider charities you'll want to benefit and the portion of your estate to leave to each.

As to each bequest, you will want to consider whether to leave it to the beneficiary outright, or whether — with the help of an expert — you will set up a trust. When you choose to use a trust, you designate a person as "trustee," and/or a bank or trust company to manage the assets in the trust, for specified uses and purposes. The trustee is then in charge of investing the assets and making distributions to the beneficiaries. For example, if you have children from a prior marriage, you may want to consider leaving any bequest to your current spouse in trust, rather than outright. Then you can have the trust terms direct that the balance (or a specified portion of the balance) remaining at your spouse's death must pass to those children, taking away your spouse's ability to give it to someone else. In the case of a bequest to a child, you will want to consider whether the child is sufficiently mature and prudent to properly manage the bequest, or whether it is preferable to leave the bequest in trust for the child, until the child attains a specified age.

If you have a substantial amount of life insurance, you may wish to consider creating a "life insurance trust." With this vehicle, during your lifetime, you would transfer the ownership of the policy to a trustee you designate as the owner of the policy. On your death, this technique will allow you to avoid estate taxes on the insurance proceeds.

A revocable "living (for management) trust" is another option, and also may help you avoid the probate process. Under this strategy, you transfer property and other assets into a trust during your lifetime, with the proviso that you can revoke it any time during your life. You can designate yourself as the trustee and select someone else to take over later, in the event you become incapacitated, or no longer want to handle your own finances. After you die, the trustee continues as manager and distributes the property to your heirs. Unfortunately, this type of trust does not avoid estate taxes.

Other key documents

1. *Durable power of attorney.* This gives another person of your choosing legal authority to manage your financial affairs if you become unable to do so. Otherwise, if you become incapacitated without a durable power of attorney, a court proceeding may be required to declare you incompetent and have a guardian appointed to manage your assets. Such a proceeding could be cumbersome, expensive, and emotionally difficult.

2. *A living will.* This document (a.k.a. an advance directive, or health-care proxy) expresses your medical wishes when you can no longer speak for yourself, and can designate someone to make your medical decisions if you cannot. A properly executed living will can avoid the litigation and distress so highly publicized, recently, in the Florida case of Terri Schiavo.

3. *Detailed letters.* Finally, it may be desirable to prepare a letter to a close relative or confidant — setting forth your wishes regarding funeral arrangements. Another letter might go to your designated executor, listing your assets and the location of documents regarding those assets, such as bank passbooks; life insurance policies; safe-deposit boxes, if any; along with the location of your will, and the names, addresses, and telephone numbers of your advisers and beneficiaries.

Review your estate plan every five years or so, or whenever there is a significant lifestyle or financial change in your circumstances. Also review your plan if there is a change in the laws regarding preparation of these documents, or the laws governing gift and estate taxes.

36

Rethink your insurance strategy

Let your emotional life drive your financial life by taking the time to do an "emotional checkup."

by Richard Bailey

Richard Bailey is a "Crystal Eagle" representative at Woodbury Financial Services, a division of The Hartford, as well as a Baptist minister, based in Ada, Oklahoma. Mr. Bailey has been helping clients meet their insurance and financial needs for 45 years.

Age 60 looks much different today than it looked 20, or even ten, years ago. Today's 60-year-old is changing the definition of retirement. People are continuing, rather than ending, their professional careers. They are contributing to society rather than withdrawing into the background. And due to advancements in health care, many 60-somethings are finding themselves in between generations rather than the oldest generation in the family. These trends mean both good and bad news for today's 60-year-old. Age 60 can be the start of the best years of our lives, but only if we are prepared for them.

I believe that financial planning should be an ongoing process throughout the various stages of life, not something to wake up one day and decide to do. The tragedy befalling many of us is that we become so overwhelmed with the prospect of planning for our financial future that we do nothing. Days turn into weeks, weeks turn into months, months turn into years, and before you know it you are unprepared when you turn 60. Many 50-somethings just give up because they feel so overwhelmed with their prospects. I urge you to put a plan in place and prioritize and tweak the plan over time so you have avenues and not dead ends in the future.

As you approach 60, I recommend taking four simple, yet powerful, steps to assess whether you'll live the final stage of your life according to your dreams and not your fears — I call this an "emotional checkup." These straightforward steps require complete honesty and communication, within ourselves and with others.

1. *Take inventory.* Many people cannot begin to list all their assets on one piece of paper, but this is needed to plan for the rest of your life. What are your financial assets, such as retirement funds, pension plans, and personal savings? What are your nonfinancial assets,

such as a car, a home, a vacation home, etc.? Then, importantly, what are your personal assets? Sixty-year-olds today touch many generations: parents, children, and grandchildren. Each person in your life should be viewed as an asset which plays a role in your financial plan. Against these assets, list potential liabilities, such as a remaining home mortgage, debts, medical bills, etc. Your loved ones of various generations may represent a potential liability if they require some sort of financial support.

2. *Decide what you want.* We must be honest about our desired lifestyle post-60 in order to plan for it properly. It is a very personal process. What will make you happy? You may be happy living a quiet life in the mountains, or you may want to live high on the hog. You need to decide how high on the hog you want to go. Depending on your desired lifestyle in retirement and your level of retirement assets, you may be able to afford the life you want. Or you may need to downsize, selling a large primary residence, buying a more manageable residence, and putting the difference to work. You also must decide what role you want to play in your loved ones' lives. You may want to financially support a child with special needs or help pay for a grandchild's college education. Or your aging parents may need special assistance. Every situation is different, and we

can't meet our financial goals until we have identified our personal goals.

3. *Protect what you have.* Once you've established your desired retirement lifestyle and identified your necessary monthly budget, you need to protect your nest egg so it will last for your lifetime, and if desired, you can pass something on to your heirs. There are insurance products that can help offset some of the major retirement risks. Life insurance can be one way to help cover remaining financial responsibilities to loved ones when you die. Permanent (or whole) life insurance can provide a financial base for those who are dependent on your income. And term life insurance can be used to cover remaining ongoing expenses your income is covering if you are still working. These might include funding remaining payments on a mortgage or ongoing expenses to support aging parents. Proper counseling can determine whether whole or term life insurance is right for you. Deferred or immediate annuities are another type of insurance product that can provide a guaranteed level of retirement income you cannot outlive. Many variable annuities also come with a guaranteed death benefit. Finally, long-term care insurance can be an effective way to prepare for unforeseen medical and assisted living or nursing home costs. Age 60, when you are usually still healthy,

is a good time to apply for long-term care insurance if you haven't already. But, of course, every situation is different, and you should seek a professional to determine what makes sense for you.

4. *Seek trusted counsel.* With my clients as with my congregation, I've found that you can't really help someone until you really understand what drives him or her. Financial planning can be very complex, and even a little scary. That's why it is important to work with a trusted financial professional who understands both people and products. A professional will help you assess what you have, decide what you want, and figure out how to get it. Respect and honor are important things for everyone, and we need to live our lives to the fullest potential. To do so, we must always remember that our emotional lives should drive our financial lives, not the other way around.

Section Six

THIS OLD HEART OF MINE

(Isley Brothers, 1966)

37

Get your 100,000-mile tune-up

You bring your car into the shop after 100,000 miles. Isn't it time to bring yourself in for your own six-decade checkup?

by Evan Appelbaum, M.D.

Evan Appelbaum, M.D., a cardiologist actively involved in patient care, teaching, and research, believes in a well-rounded, balanced life to foster and maintain health. He calls music his "ultimate form of relaxation" and jams on his guitar with a group several times a month. Dr. Appelbaum says that the marathon sessions leave him feeling focused and energetic, "a testament to the degree of joy" he's experienced.

How do you respond whenever anyone asks, "How are you?" Probably, you answer, "Fine." But are you really "fine?"

Joan thought she was. Oh, maybe she'd had an occasional ache or pain, but she'd chalked it up to turning 60.

Whoa! Being 60 doesn't mean putting up with an ache or a pain. "Quality of life" is what we aim for nowadays, and one day, I suspect, instead of greeting people with, "How are you?," we'll say, "How's your quality of life?" That's what is really important. It's the first thing that comes into my mind when someone steps into my office. If you're 60, even if your answer is, "Fine," having a checkup is a good idea.

Think of a car. Even though it's functioning well enough, you still bring it in for its 100,000-mile tune-up. Isn't your body worth the same kind of attention?

In fact, Joan probably would have put up with her aches and pains and never come in to see me at all, if a news article hadn't caught her attention when she was tooling around the Internet one day. She read that after menopause, a woman's estrogen levels — which had been protecting her heart — drop, and she becomes more prone to coronary disease. Joan went to see her primary doctor, and he sent her to me. I'm a cardiologist.

The woman who walked into my office looked healthy, and in fact, Joan told me she felt healthy. If she were a car, she would have been the car a little old lady drives once a week — to go to church.

She sat down, we talked, and I evaluated her to identify any risk factors. Joan said she didn't smoke or drink, and had no strong family history of heart disease. When I ran some blood tests, though, we found that she had mild hypertension and high levels of low-density lipoprotein (LDL), or what we call "bad" cholesterol. Joan was also moderately overweight, and when she confessed to being a couch potato, we sat down again and talked about her diet.

She lived alone and, as is often the case with people who live alone, Joan tended to skip meals and replace them with snacks, such as chips and high-fat dips, that were easy to eat in front of the TV. I told her to go home and clean out her refrigerator, and gave her a list of no-no's to toss: butter, chips, and anything with trans fats.

"Keep your glasses handy when you shop," I said, "and read the labels. Fill your refrigerator with fresh fruits and vegetables, lean meat, chicken, fish, and some whole-grain products." To raise her "good" cholesterol, or high-density lipoprotein (HDL), I advised her to use olive oil generously on her salads and snack on nuts.

The next step was to get Joan off that couch. I wanted her to exercise, but nothing strenuous at first, and suggested that she walk for a half hour, three or four times a week.

After three months, Joan came back with some good results. She'd lost weight and her blood pressure had normalized. Her cholesterol levels were still not good, however, and I placed her on a statin medicine to help lower the bad cholesterol. By Joan's next checkup, her levels were better, and she surprised me by telling me she wanted to join a gym. We performed a stress test, and when she passed with flying colors, I "green lighted" her for the gym.

John: The heavy-duty car

John was a different story. Like Joan, he had recently passed his 60th birthday, but he was the car who had done extra-duty work — and his body showed it. While out shoveling snow, he'd developed chest pains, and his primary doctor had sent him to me.

I evaluated John. He had high blood pressure and was overweight. John had what we call "apple-shaped obesity" — with the weight centrally located in a paunch, or beer gut (unlike "pear-shaped obesity" — where the weight is located lower, around the hips and buttocks).

Tests showed that he was a borderline diabetic, which is a red flag. Diabetes is often a major cause of hypertension and heart disease. I recommended a stress test and it turned out positive, showing significant coronary problems and a blockage in the main artery.

John was quickly scheduled for surgery and a balloon angioplasty. Then we talked. I explained that he had to make some lifestyle changes, and he agreed at once — he'd had a scare. "Cut out the beer," was the first thing I said. I put John on an aggressive diet to lose weight, while still keeping his hunger satisfied. For exercise, I suggested leaving the car at home and walking to his office, which was about a mile away.

He was a good patient; he lost weight, his blood pressure levels came down, and he kept up his exercising — walking longer distances during the week and going for hikes on weekends. John did so well, we decided that he could have an occasional glass of — no, not beer, but heart-healthy red wine with his evening meal.

Both Joan and John are in good shape now. I always think it's a shame when people have to get a scare before they do what they should have done in the first place. To ensure the quality of your life, schedule your 100,000-mile tune-up today!

38

Get physical

No pain, no gain! Exercise is "sorely" needed — to keep you fit and happy for the rest of your life.

by Edward G. McFarland, M.D.

Edward G. McFarland, M.D., established the Division of Sports Medicine and Shoulder Surgery at the Johns Hopkins Medical Institutions in Baltimore, Maryland, in 1992. He is a professor of orthopedic surgery at the Johns Hopkins University School of Medicine. Dr. McFarland, who played football at Murray State University in Kentucky (and "was rarely injured"), now says that he "gets sore more often than he would like to admit" when playing *any* sport with his three daughters.

The bad news about being 60 is that you realize that the things the experts (and your parents) once said about your health are correct. Things like "eat the right foods" and "get plenty of exercise and sleep" will prolong your life and make you feel happier, more energetic, even frisky. They will also keep you living longer and more independently, which may not seem that important now, but will — over the next two or three decades of your life.

If you don't exercise, start now — even if all you do is walk around the mall. The Surgeon General and the American College of Sports Medicine recommend at least 30 minutes of exercise, three times a week, preferably every day. Studies have shown that you'll feel better, have fewer health problems, and very likely lose weight. What's more, we know that it's easier to keep your weight down with exercise. An added plus is that the more you exercise, the greater the effect on your health — both mental and physical. It might even help your sex life, according to some experts.

Unfortunately, what's also true is that all your past injuries from sports or other causes can come back to haunt you, and perhaps restrict your activity. The other bad news is that if you exercise, you'll probably have some new aches and pains.

Be aware that there is "good pain" and "bad pain." Let me explain. At 60, things tend to hurt. As a maturing Baby Boomer myself, I feel your pain. It seems as if I'm trying to get into shape every two weeks or so, with the expected soreness and aches that come with intermittent exercise. The old axiom, "If you don't use it, you'll lose it," has a corollary: "If you don't use it very often, it will hurt some, after you do."

Here are a couple of caveats. Before you begin an exercise program, get clearance from your medical doctor, especially if there's a history of heart disease in your family. If you have any problems with your joints or bones, consult your physical therapist or trainer to determine what exercises you should or should not perform.

Remember, there is a difference between fatigue, pain, and soreness. After you exercise, you should feel a little exhilarated and tired. This fatigue should be temporary, lasting a few minutes or hours. You may also feel a "burn" in your muscles, bones, and joints from what we call low-grade stress; this "good pain" is a sign that your exercise is pushing you a little and helping you gain strength and endurance. The burn should be short-lived, however, and not continue after exercising, or interfere with your activities or sleep.

If your muscles, bones, and joints see too much stress over a short period, they will react by getting sore. Soreness is pain that occurs with, or after, exercise for hours, or even days. It can occur whenever you begin a new activity or increase an activity too much or too fast. This "bad pain" is a sign that your body has had too much activity. Another sign is swelling, which happens in joints that have wear and tear of the cartilage (i.e., that have some arthritis). Bones that see too much stress will hurt with any weight-bearing exercise, even walking. Stressed muscles will be sore for 24 to 48 hours after exercise, a condition known as "delayed-onset muscle soreness," since you don't realize right away that you've overdone it.

There are ways to cope with "good pain" and "bad pain." If you have a little discomfort, either the same day, or the day after exercising, cut back on the activity. Instead of two sets of tennis, play one. To avoid stiffness of the joints, stretch the involved muscles and joints to maintain your range of motion. Try placing ice for 20 to 30 minutes on the area that hurts (unless you've been warned not to use cold on the skin).

If the pain hurts enough to use medicine, it's generally recommended that you start with acetaminophen, using it only as outlined in the instructions. Too much can hurt your liver, a vital organ. If you are not on blood thinners and don't have a history of stomach ulcers, reflux disease, bleeding ulcers, ulcerative colitis, kidney or liver damage or transplant, then the use of over-the-counter nonsteroidal, anti-inflammatory drugs may be of benefit. However, these medications have serious side effects and should be taken only after checking with your physician.

"Good pain" typically eases and fades away with rest, ice, and perhaps the use of one of these medicines, on a limited basis.

"Bad pain" gets worse with more activity. It's important to rest and let the injured area recover. Usually, the soreness will ease and disappear entirely, but if it doesn't, and the simple measures I've mentioned don't help, then you should seek help from a medical professional. Once a diagnosis is made, you'll be told what exercises you can or cannot do.

For example, if you have arthritis in your knee, then avoid exercises that put weight on the leg. If you can walk without pain and swelling, then walking may be fine. The best exercises eliminate gravity, such as cycling, swimming, and to a lesser degree, elliptical trainers. If you cycle, avoid hills and keep to level ground, with the seat adjusted as high as possible.

Tendonitis is an irritation of a tendon, a structure that connects muscles to bones. Treatment for an irritated tendon is the same as for an irritated joint: rest, ice, range of motion, and maybe a short course of medication. The most common areas for inflammation are the rotator-cuff tendons in the shoulder; the tendons on the outside of the elbow (also called tennis elbow); and the Achilles tendon, behind the heel of your foot. In any joint, it's important to maintain your range of motion by stretching. Typically, if you have tendonitis in one joint, you can still exercise your other joints.

These guidelines are important for trying to stay active, fit, and happy. Everyone gets a little tired and sore after exercise, but if you don't recover with the suggestions outlined above, a visit to a health-care professional may be in your best interest. If old injuries flare up, with caution, you can work around them. Remember, you are only in your 60s, and while aches and pains may occur with activity, most of them can be managed to allow you to be healthy, happy, and active.

39

Treat yourself like a star

Follow this natural-nutrition and wrinkle-control program to rejuvenate your skin and boost your energy level. You'll be ready to rock 'n' roll in no time!

by Nicholas V. Perricone, M.D.

Nicholas Perricone, M.D., is a board-certified clinical and research dermatologist (a.k.a. as The Wrinkle King). He is the author of five *New York Times* best sellers, including *Forever Young, The Perricone Weight Loss Diet, The Perricone Prescription, The Clear Skin Prescription,* and *The Wrinkle Cure.*

As someone who came of age in the late '60s, I believe that some of the best popular music was created during those turbulent years. The Who, one of the leading bands of that decade, penned and sang a rallying cry for our generation with the song line, "I hope I die before I get old!" in the 1966 song, "My Generation." Luckily for Pete Townshend and us, this wish has not yet come true. He is going strong and still touring to sold-out crowds, like other bands from that era.

Recently, I heard directly from a member of one of those bands, and I readily admit to feeling a bit of a thrill that one of the most famous rock icons of my generation contacted me.

"Dr. Perricone, I need help," Rick (not his real name) said. "I have a sold-out tour looming on the horizon and my energy levels are pretty low. Sure, once on stage, the adrenaline kicks in (and no doubt other helpful stimulants, too! I thought). But I have to be ready for all of the rest that touring entails."

Rick spent a lot of time in the islands, where he had a palatial estate worthy of his world-class rock-star status. When he wasn't sitting by his pool, he was out on his sailboat. Consequently, his skin had suffered a significant amount of sun damage and wrinkling. Although he had dropped many bad habits, including chain smoking, he was no saint, and years of life in the fast lane were taking their toll.

Rick was also somewhat of a legend when it came to women, and was currently dating a very young model — additional motivation for him to get going on a rejuvenation program.

"So, Doc, what's first?" he asked. "When do I go under the knife?"

"That's not the answer, Rick," I told him. "We're going to do this the 'natural' way." Since he was also a child of the '60s, I was hoping that this holistic approach would appeal to him. "First, you have to start with an anti-inflammatory diet and supplement program, which will be a great help for overall energy and stamina," I advised. Then, we introduce the fun parts of the rejuvenation process, like working with some cool substances — biochemicals that we researchers know as neuropeptides."

I knew Rick would be one of the all-time challenges of my career. As a physician and educator, I enjoy healing and teaching. When I was in medical school, I discovered that inflammation was present in both aging skin and the disease process. I have also learned the key causes of this inflammation — environmental stressors, physical stress, and poor diet, with diet being the most culpable. To combat the effects of the inflammation, I started Rick on a total skin-and-body nutritional program and topical antioxidant products—or what I call a three-tiered program.

Tier One

The anti-inflammatory diet, which should consist of the following:

- High-quality protein, such as that found in fish, shell-fish, poultry, and tofu.

• Low-glycemic carbohydrates, including colorful fresh fruits and vegetables, whole grains such as old-fashioned oatmeal, and legumes, such as beans and lentils.
• Healthy fats, such as those found in cold water fish (especially wild Alaskan salmon, halibut, sardines, herring, and anchovies), nuts, seeds, and olive oil.
• 8–10 glasses of pure spring water per day.
• Antioxidant rich beverages, such as green tea.

Tier Two

A wide variety of unique nutritional supplements. My research has shown that nutrients that possess antioxidant properties act as natural anti-inflammatories. Designed to work synergistically with the anti-inflammatory diet, these nutrients offer anti-aging, anti-inflammatory, fat-metabolizing, and brain-energizing benefits. They also help prevent and reverse oxidative damage on a cellular level — of critical importance as we age. My favorite antioxidide nutrients include: alpha lipoic acid, vitamin C ester, DMAE (dimethyl amino ethanol), coenzme Q-10, conjugated linoleic acid (GLA), L-carmine fumerate, glutamine, omega-3 essential fatty acids, carnosine, benfotiamine, and astaxanthin.

Tier Three

Topical antioxidants in creams and lotions that work synergistically with diet and supplements. As a dermatologist, I love working with topical elements because the results can be visible so quickly! The following substances have been shown to significantly improve the appearance of skin when added to topical formulations: alpha lipoic acid, DMAE (dimethyl amino ethanol), neuropeptides, olive oil polyphenols, phisphatidycholine, vitamin C ester, and astaxanthin.

I didn't see Rick for four weeks. One day I received two tickets to Rick's kickoff concert at Madison Square Garden — along with a couple of backstage passes. After a quick mental lament on what these tickets would have meant to my popularity a couple of decades ago, I drove into the city. I was looking forward to the show, but nothing quite prepared me for the spectacle that unfolded over the next three hours. Rick and the group performed with the drive and energy of 16-year-olds — and the screaming fans kept up an equally impressive performance.

Backstage with Rick, I could see immediately that his newfound energy was the result of his past four weeks on the program. His skin glowed. His lines and wrinkles appeared to have much less depth, and overall, his skin appeared more smooth and supple.

"I want to thank you, Doc," he smiled. "I feel like a new man." And, truth be told, he looked like one, too.

As Rick's story proves, the news is good for us baby boomers. For decades, my colleagues and I have been researching ways to slow down the aging clock. We boomers will never go gracefully. We will fight it every step of the way.

Try my three-tiered program. Remember that sugars and starchy foods are your worst enemy — they elevate your blood sugar and insulin levels, thereby accelerating aging and disease, breaking down muscle mass, and preventing your body from burning fat. Learning how to control your blood sugar and insulin levels (and the resultant inflammation) is the greatest antiaging secret there is. This is a simple formula accessible to all — in fact, everything you need is available online or at the health food store.

Our generation may be the first generation to be eternally, perpetually young. And who knows? Without a crystal ball to peer into the future, we have no idea what direction our lives will take. Perhaps, like jazz legend Eubie Blake, you'll be forming your own record company at the age of 90. Or, like our friend Rick, you'll be performing live at Madison Square Garden to a crowd of adoring fans half your age!

40

Cherish every day

When you've been to death's door, life truly becomes precious. You cherish simple things, such as sapphire skies with wispy clouds and fragrant flowers. You live every day as if it is your last.

by Mellanie True Hills

Mellanie True Hills is a heart disease survivor, heart health expert, patient advocate, award-winning author, and founder and CEO of the non-profit American Foundation for Women's Health and StopAfib.org, the world's foremost atrial fibrillation patient advocacy organization. She is the author of *A Woman's Guide to Saving Her Own Life: The HEART Program for Health and Longevity*. She received an American Heart Association Outstanding Advocate Award and speaks at the organization's Go Red for Women events. Find out more at http://www.mellaniehills.com.

At age 51, my life changed dramatically when I experienced symptoms of a heart attack. Women rarely get the crushing chest pains that men do, and instead are more likely to experience shortness of breath, indigestion, nausea, fatigue, or pain in the left arm, shoulder, jaw, or elsewhere in the left side of the body. I had shortness of breath and pain in my left shoulder, and was treated for a heart attack.

I was lucky to have recognized my symptoms in time, and thus didn't have a heart attack, but I was probably only minutes away from one. I had a 95 percent blockage in a major coronary artery, and almost died on the operating table — but I received a second chance.

Many women aren't as lucky, since women's symptoms are subtle and easily missed. You may not think about women having heart attacks, but surprisingly more women than men die from heart disease. Heart disease — not breast cancer — is a woman's No. 1 risk, but the great news is that we now understand much more about women's heart disease.

Take care of you

My doctors were stunned because I didn't have the usual heart disease risk factors — no smoking, diabetes, high cholesterol, or high blood pressure (mine was low). We thought there might be family history, but my doctors have discounted that, too. I was simply overweight and overstressed, like many of us. At the time, stress wasn't considered a risk factor, but we now know that it is.

Women tend to care for everyone else first, and take on everyone else's stress. We must put ourselves first to protect our health.

Here's my simple five-step plan for living to 100. Yes, even heart disease survivors can aspire to that. This plan can work for you, too.

1. *Control your stress.* Start here, because hyperbusy life styles put you at risk — once you control your stress hormones, these other steps are easy.

2. *Get enough sleep and relaxation.* If you get at least 7–8 hours sleep per night, plus naps if you wish, and take vacations, you'll protect your health.

3. *Eat right.* Eat fruits, vegetables, and grains. Have the good fats in moderation, and avoid or minimize the bad fats. This helped me lose 85 pounds. If necessary, lose weight.

4. *Exercise every day.* Take that 30-to-60-minute walk every day to strengthen your heart, and do weight-bearing exercise at least twice a week to keep your muscles strong.

5. *Take proactive control of your health.* Educate yourself on health and partner with your health-care provider. Know your risk factors and control them.

One more thing — if you smoke, stopping will add years to your life.

Sixty is not too late — it's never really too late — to make changes to optimize your health. As Albert Einstein said, "The clever person solves a problem; the wise person avoids it." Do these things for 21 days and you'll have healthy habits to ensure a long, vital life.

What will you do with the rest of your life?

Getting a second chance makes you ponder your mortality, which may lead to changes as you seek answers and new meaning from life. It meant starting over for me.

First, changing jobs. I left my corporate road-warrior job, where I made a difference for companies, so that I could start making a difference for people. I now use my second chance for speaking and writing to spread the word about how to avoid heart disease by living a healthy life.

Second, changing pace. We moved to the country, slowed down, and simplified to enjoy every precious day. We now enjoy nature, wide open spaces, and beautiful views.

As I traveled around the country speaking, a woman named Mary was in my audience one day. She recognized herself in my story, and her doctor found that she has heart disease. Mary now has a second chance at life.

By reading this, you have a second chance, too. I hope you will use it to ponder these questions, which may alter your life. Take time to go into the silence of your mind — tune out distractions and sit quietly — to consider:

- What have I always dreamed but haven't done? What's stopping me? How can I do it?
- Am I making a difference in the world?
- What do I want to accomplish by the time my days are through? Do I have a written plan to get there?
- Am I taking care of my health? Do I have a written plan for it?
- Am I putting myself first? If I don't, who will? Will I be there to care for those I love, and to see my grand children, or great-grandchildren?
- Do I have the resources to carry out my dreams? How can I handle the unexpected — medical bills, job change, or even disability?
- Just in case, are my affairs in order?
- Have I told those I love today that I love them?

As we reach 60, we boomers are not over the hill — we have always changed the world, so should being 60 and beyond be any different? Sure, some things creak, but we're wiser, more caring, loving, and maybe even sexier. We have the wisdom to know where to invest our energy to make the biggest impact.

We may be just beginning the second half of our lives. We won't reach 120, but could easily reach 100 and beyond, and have ahead of us as many years as we have worked. Medical science continues to help us live longer, if we do our part.

This can be the best time of your life. How can you ensure that you can fulfill your dreams? Make a commitment right now by writing, and then saying out loud, today and every day: *I cherish each day, I take care of me, and I make a difference.*

41

Be a mover and a shaker

Despite the diagnosis of a progressive disease, such as Parkinson's, never waver in your resolve to enjoy life to the fullest! Keep your eye on the road ahead and enjoy the journey.

by Charles Faulkner Bryan, Jr.

Charles Faulkner Bryan, Jr., holds a Ph.D. in history, and is a distinguished public historian having served as President and chief executive officer of the Virginia Historical Society for 20 years (1988-2008). Dr. Bryan has published extensively on a variety of subjects in American history and museum management. A frequent consultant at museums throughout the United States, he has served as president of the American Association for State & Local History and was on the board of the Smithsonian's National Museum of American History.

When I was a teenager, I took my hand-me-down car to a mechanic our family had used since the days of Model-T Fords. To me, he was an old man, although now I realize that he must have been about 60. He loved to regale me with homespun philosophy. People are just like cars, he declared. Even our parts eventually break down.

I learned this was true when my father had a massive heart attack when he was only 42. I was eight. To stall the breakdown process in my own life, I became a fitness fanatic. Even when I passed my own 42nd birthday, bettering my father's life span, I kept to my rigid fitness regime.

When I turned 50, I swelled with pride when my family physician declared he'd be out of a job if more of his patients were as healthy and fit as I was. Though my "car" was accruing digits on its odometer, I had taken good care of myself and was running smoothly.

Then, I began to detect a slight vibration. Just after my 57th birthday, I started noticing little things that I initially dismissed as fatigue, stress, and simply aging. I had been running three miles or more daily for years, for instance, but was now unable to finish that last mile. And I noticed a slight tremor in my right hand. My handwriting had never been good, but the characters I now put to paper looked like the shaky crawl of a really old man.

My movements became more deliberate and rigid, while a slight hesitation showed up in my speech. Sometimes, my words were slurred. My wife asked me why I dragged my right foot when I walked or why I didn't swing my arms anymore. Even my face began to lack expression, making me appear tired and bored.

It was time to visit the garage for a checkup.

I was unprepared for my doctor's early diagnosis: a brain tumor, a stroke . . . or Parkinson's disease (PD). When PD was confirmed, my wife and I broke down in tears, terrified at what the future held for us. We began to read everything we could. We learned that Parkinson's is a breakdown in the brain's ability to coordinate messages to the muscles, eventually resulting in difficulty walking, dressing, eating, speaking — essentially any type of body movement. We learned that symptoms can be diminished for extended periods with drug treatment and physical therapy. And, we learned that while Parkinson's is not fatal, as yet there is no cure.

I plunged into severe depression, sure I would have to give up a job I loved, and that I would become an invalid and a burden to my family. Yet, nearly two years later, despite the steady progress of my disease, I have attained a state of peace. The strong support I've received from my family and colleagues have been key factors. Getting on the right medication, a tricky business with Parkinson's, has also helped immensely. But it's my positive attitude and determination not to give up, I think, that has made the most difference. Here are the daily rules I now live by:

1. *Be open about what ails you.* I decided, early on, to go public with my Parkinson's. Michael J. Fox, perhaps the most famous person with the disease, confessed that one of the biggest mistakes he ever made was his decade-long attempt to conceal his affliction. All too many people with disorders like PD are reluctant to admit their diagnosis outside a small circle of family and friends, either out of shame or fear of losing their job. Because of the high public profile of my job, I knew it would be impossible to disguise the manifestations of my disease. From the onset, I decided to be open. Soon after my diagnosis, I told my colleagues at work. Now, when I speak in public, something I do often, I tell my audience up front. And, as I struggle to endorse a check at the bank, I let the teller know what's taking me so long. I have found that being open about Parkinson's not only makes me less uptight, it helps make the people I'm dealing with feel more comfortable.

2. *Use humor to ease the burden.* Laughter is the best way I've found to put myself and others at ease. Last year, I started monthly breakfast meetings with two friends who also have Parkinson's. I suggested we call ourselves "The Movers and Shakers." Busting out in laughter, we agreed the name was perfect. I have found a whole new meaning to the truism, "If I couldn't laugh, I'd cry."

3. *Don't obsess over your ailment and don't bore others with it.* Older people spend an inordinate amount of time talking about their health. Eavesdrop on a group of seniors, and inevitably the conversation turns to somebody's hip replacement. Early in my Parkinson's, I rarely missed an opportunity to work it into the conversation. Then, I sat next to a man at a dinner party who spent much of the evening talking in great detail about his recent open- heart surgery. Obviously, it was the most important subject in his life at the time, but his obsession became my boredom. People may be sorry about your condition, but there's a limit to their patience in listening.

4. *Stay active and productive as long as you can.* This is hardly an earth-shaking revelation, but it is especially true for anyone who wrestles with an incurable disease. Soon after my diagnosis, I struggled with the thought of early retirement. And I was tempted to withdraw from the world. Eating in public, for example, can be an awkward and embarrassing experience; soups, spaghetti, and salads are big no-no's! But as my doctor reminded me, every day I don't work out or go to the office, the Parkinson's wins.

This old car has been hitting many potholes over the last several miles. My tires wobble; my engine has a pronounced knock. And when I push the accelerator, the response is sluggish. Still, I'm not ready to pull off the road, yet! With a steady eye on the path before me and both hands tightly gripping the wheel, I'm determined to enjoy the miles ahead. Parkinson's has helped me to learn that I can handle what life throws me — if I have the right attitude.

42

Sleep tight

You've probably slept a total of 20 years over the past six decades, the same length of time that the title character snoozed in Washington Irving's *Rip Van Winkle*. Since you literally sleep to live, learn to sleep well!

by Gerard Lombardo, M.D.

Gerard Lombardo, M.D., is the founder and director of the Center for Sleep Disorders Medicine & Research at the New York Methodist Hospital in Brooklyn, New York. He considers the raising of his four children, with his wife, celebrity chef and cookbook author Daisy Martinez, to be life's greatest challenge. A close second, he says, is "reducing his golf handicap to less than ten." Dr. Lombardo coauthored, with Henry Ehrlich, the book *Sleep to Save Your Life*.

Sleep is an important investment in time and should be treated that way. Some of the rules for good sleep hygiene, such as avoiding caffeine in the evening, are obvious and have been taught to us by our parents. Others, such as steering clear of heavy meals, alcohol, and nicotine too close to bedtime, are not so obvious and are learned by trial and error. Medication can also disturb your sleep and, if you're having problems, you should discuss any side effects with your doctor, who can suggest changes.

Other good sleep hygiene measures

1. Keep your bedroom comfortable, dark, and quiet. (Yes, that means if you have an office in your bedroom, move it and the TV to another room.)
2. Observe a regular schedule, with an early rise time and exposure to sunlight whenever possible, and a reasonable, regular bedtime.
3. Get seven to eight hours of sleep each night, and if you must nap, keep it under 30 minutes.
4. Stay busy! All too often, in my practice, I see problems caused by sedentary and nonproductive days. Long naps in front of a TV, with no social interaction, often lead to insomnia, even if that behavior is limited to weekends or vacations. An active and rewarding day will have you begging for the pillow at night.

As years go by

Advancing age does not, by itself, disturb our need or desire for sleep. For some fortunate few, perfect sleep is the rule, but for about one-fourth of Americans, ages 50 to 59, a good sleep has to be earned — by understanding and following the rules.

Physiology also plays a role. As we age, our sleep changes in quantity and quality. REM, or dream sleep, stays about the same, but there's a decrease in the amount of deep sleep, stages three and four, and an increase in light sleep. Growth-hormone production decreases and levels of cortisol, a stress hormone, fluctuate in response to poor sleep and the physical discomforts from the daily wear and tear. The overall result is lighter stages of sleep and less restorative sleep.

Things can get even more complicated. If we try to compensate for diminishing sleep quality, the sleep thief, known affectionately as a nap, starts to steal precious hours from our nighttime sleep, resulting in insomnia, an inability to get to sleep or stay asleep. While we're struggling to stay awake the next day, we may go on a caffeine binge with cola and/or coffee, and perhaps take another nap. We're caught in a vicious cycle, and if it continues, it can cause long-term damage.

The ABCs of sleep disorders

Even if the rules are followed, some 70 sleep disorders have been identified that become more common as we grow older. These include:

1. Disordered breathing, such as snoring or sleep-apnea syndrome. The Greek word *apnea* means "without breath." People with sleep apnea stop breathing repeatedly during sleep. Twelve million Americans suffer from

this syndrome which, if untreated, can cause high blood pressure, stroke, heart attack, diabetes, and depression. The disruption of restorative sleep may result in excessive sleepiness during the day, job impairment, and accidents.

2. Restless leg syndrome while awake or leg-movement disorder during sleep. Ten to 30 percent of 50- to 59-year-olds suffer from this disorder. Often, the cause can be traced to iron deficiency, anemia, or caffeine overuse, and can be treated by lifestyle changes and/or medication.

Diagnosing a sleep disorder

If you wake up mentally and physically unrefreshed and feel sleepy all day, chances are you have a sleep disorder. Your bed partner may have witnessed symptoms, such as snoring, gasping, pauses in breathing, or thrashing about and restlessness. You may have noticed memory loss during the day, a lack of concentration, and some job impairment.

Your next step: report any symptoms to your doctor. At this time, there is no specific blood test to screen for poor sleep (although research is ongoing), but the doctor can probably identify (or diagnose) the problem by discussing your symptoms. In the last decade, researchers have come up with a number of treatments for sleep disorders, including surgery to open air passages; oral devices to use when you sleep, which will help to keep the airway open; medication; and lifestyle changes, such as diet and exercise.

Sleep is recognized as the final frontier for good health — joining diet and exercise as part of an overall plan. Whether you are working full-time or part-time, or are retired, the quality of your life will increase as you meet the challenges of a changing body and spirit. If you think about what you eat and how to stay active and fit, all that is left is to plan for and think about a good quality of sleep. The three work together.

A recent survey of centenarians showed that the majority had a positive outlook and peaceful demeanor. Why not incorporate this attitude not only into your awake period, but also into a carefully thought-out practice of good sleep?

You spend one-third of your life sleeping! If you're planning to have a productive and healthy next decade, you should have about three years of good sleep during that time. To live long and happily, sleep well!

43

Be comprehensive with your health

Before you choose a therapy, research natural and prescription therapies with your doctor. Be a healthy — and happy — patient!

by Jacob Teitelbaum, M.D.

Jacob Teitelbaum, M.D., an internist, dropped out of medical school for one year, in 1975, because of chronic fatigue syndrome (CFS). He cured himself with herbs and alternative healing therapies. Today he is nationally known expert in the fields of chronic fatigue syndrome, fibromyalgia, sleep and pain. The senior author of the landmark study, "Effective Treatment of Chronic Fatigue Syndrome and Fibromyalgia," Dr. Teitelbaum also wrote *The Fatigue and Fibromyalgia Solution, From Fatigued to Fantastic, Three Steps to Happiness! Real Cause, Real Cure, Healing Through Joy, Beat Sugar Addiction NOW!* and *Pain Free 1-2-3!*

The bumper sticker has it right when it says, "This is not a dress rehearsal — Live life NOW!" So many of us responsibly planned, saved, and sacrificed for the future that we forgot how to have fun. Well, guess what?

If you're approaching or past 60, now is the future for which you sacrificed. It's time to relearn how to have fun!

I'll let you in on a few secrets I've learned in my 29 years as a physician. First of all, it's hard to make happy people sick, and if they get an illness, they usually sail through it. Studies have even shown that people with diabetes and angina patients who are depressed have as much as double the risk of dying during the studies' follow-up period as those who are happy!

Second, doctors mostly know what the drug companies tell them. The pharmaceutical industry pays for almost all of our conferences and journals, and if you think that doesn't affect what's taught, I've got a bridge to sell you. Fortunately, being 60, you already know better. This conflict of interest means that, despite your doctor's good intentions, he will usually recommend the newest and most expensive medications and procedures, regardless of whether there are other safer and more effective (often natural) alternatives.

So, how can you improve your outlook on life? I recommend that you start by taking a few days to see what makes you "feel good." Give your brain, and "what's practical," the day off. Make a list of those things in your life that "feel good," and those that don't. Then, decide to keep your attention on the positives, while withdrawing your energy and attention from the negatives. Also, give yourself permission to fantasize about anything that "feels good," and add those thoughts and ideas to the "keeper" list.

What about health problems — surely you can't ignore them? Actually, a lot of times, you would be better off if you did take your attention off them — except when you're actually doing something to fix the problems. Remember — it is the job of the health industry to keep you constantly worried about medical problems, so that they can sell you expensive stuff. Unfortunately, nobody pays to make sure that doctors learn about safe, highly effective, research-proven, low-cost therapies. Sadly, your well-meaning doctor often does not even know there are alternatives.

As a personal example, let me tell you about 1975, a really rough year for me. I was caught in the middle of a family meltdown while in my third year of medical school. I was 22, and my father had died years earlier, so I was paying my own way. Finally, the stress caught up with me. I had what I called the "drop-dead flu." Three months later, I was still exhausted, unable to sleep, achy all over, and "had no brain." Devastated, I had to drop out of medical school. Since I was paying my own way and relying on scholarships, student loans, and work (which I was now too sick to do), I literally found myself homeless and sleeping in parks. This was my introduction to chronic fatigue syndrome (CFS) and fibromyalgia. If I had relied on standard medical therapy, I would still be disabled. Fortunately, I met practitioners familiar with natural therapies, and was back in med school, getting honors, a year later.

The good news is that by using what I call "comprehensive medicine" — a mix of the best natural and prescription therapies — most medical problems can be effectively treated so that you feel great. This is true and scientifically proven, despite the fact that your doctor may often be clueless about these therapies (again, unless they are expensive).

Another excellent example is pain management. All your doctor is usually trained to do is to give you Motrin or Tylenol, and narcotics if you have cancer.

Here are a few examples of how effective comprehensive medicine can be. When I was waiting to go on CNN recently, a clip was aired about doing surgery to remove large sections of face muscles to prevent migraines. The clip said this procedure decreased migraines 50 percent and likely costs tens of thousands of dollars. I wanted to put my head in the studio and tell them that by taking high doses of vitamin B-2, plus some vitamin B-12 and magnesium each day (cost, approximately 20 cents), you can decrease migraines by more than 70 percent, after six weeks. This has been proven in multiple studies.

Many individuals suffer from sciatica (back pain from disc disease). Holistic doctors often use IV Colchicine (a prescription medicine) for disc disease. This has been found in repeated studies on over a thousand patients to be beneficial, and costs a total of $18 versus $27,000 for back surgery.

For arthritis pain, doctors may recommend an analgesic or Motrin to temporarily relieve the pain, but that's all they can do. Research, however, shows that a number of natural treatments found at any health food store can actually improve and heal joints. Investigate herbal remedies, like willow bark and boswellia (frankincense) on the Internet. They've been shown to be as effective as brand-name drugs after six weeks of use, but are very safe and inexpensive.

Another example is a treatment for osteoporosis. The mineral strontium has been shown in placebo-controlled studies to be more effective than most medications, yet it's safe and inexpensive.

Do your homework. Don't take any medication unless you know what you are taking, and what its side effects could be. Use the Internet as an investigative tool and a guide to possible alternative treatments. You'll find that you can treat most medical problems effectively and safely when you combine both natural and prescription therapies, and also save yourself an enormous amount of money. The same principles apply to Parkinson's Disease, high cholesterol, heart disease, and most of the other problems affecting Americans in their 60s, today.

Using the best of natural and prescription therapies, you can find yourself feeling fantastic. I routinely remind doctors at my lectures, though, that if you get people well so that they go back to a life they hate, you've done nothing for them.

Now is the time for you to follow your bliss. If not now, when?

44

Stress: the good, the bad, the ugly

If the effects of stress are becoming overwhelming, restore your health and balance by trying these four simple steps.

by Dr. Kathleen Hall, Ph.D.

National stress expert Dr. Kathleen Hall is the founder and CEO of The Stress Institute, and Mindful Living Network. She has been featured in numerous media outlets, including The Today Show, *Fortune*, *USA Today*, the *Wall Street Journal*, *Cosmopolitan*, Dr. OZ Show, Huffington Post, and *Parade*. She also is the author of four books: *Mindful Living Everyday*, *Uncommon HOPE*, *A Life in Balance: Nourishing the Four Roots of True Happiness* and *Alter Your Life: Overbooked? Overworked? Overwhelmed?*

In the 1980s, my life was in the fast lane. I had a great husband and children, a nice home, elegant clothes, and enjoyed fabulous vacations. I felt I'd grabbed my piece of the American dream. Life was moving at a well orchestrated pace when, in a split second, the dream stalled.

The elevator door opened on the 104th floor of the World Trade Center and I couldn't move. I felt paralyzed. My heart was racing, my chest so tight I couldn't breathe. Later, I would learn I was in the throes of my first debilitating panic attack.

To try to regain control of my life, I began a quest, later an intense passion, to understand stress and to discover how to create balance and true happiness. After nearly two decades of gathering research, obtaining post graduate educational degrees, and engaging in clinical trainings at research centers across the country, I founded the Stress Institute. There was a need for a credible source, where the millions suffering from stress could find scientifically backed information, research, and guidance.

I have learned to have great reverence for stress. Stress is a natural and essential part of life. It is as much a part of life as breathing, eating, and drinking. Every day, our bodies are bombarded with both negative and positive forms of stress. While negative stress can make us physically and mentally sick and unhappy, positive stress can motivate and drive us to accomplish great things.

Stress discovers our dark places, bringing them to our attention. One of the greatest lessons I have learned in life is that each stressor you perceive as an obstacle is actually an opportunity for your personal growth and happiness. The stress in my life showed me I had constructed a hollow life living other people's definitions of happiness and success. In my case, my panic attacks drove me out of a shallow life of habituation and unhappiness into a new life of purpose, balance, and happiness.

We all know the consequences of neglecting a serious wound — it gets worse. It can lead to gangrene and amputation or, worse, cost us our lives. The same goes for stress. Sadly, the phrase "stress kills" is true.

During my research, I discovered there are many ways to manage stress — even to reverse its effects. I have broken my favorite techniques into four "roots," if you will, as I believe that making them a part of your life builds a solid foundation. The acronym I use for the roots is "S.E.L.F." When we S.E.L.F. care, stress doesn't stand a chance. I know; it has worked for me!

S.E.L.F.
"S" is for serenity, the opposite of stress.

When we practice serenity, our bodies experience the relaxation response, in which blood pressure and heart rate drop. Reducing stress reduces your risk of cancer, heart disease, stroke, obesity, insomnia, diabetes, depression, and anxiety disorders.

Mini: Memorize a three- to five- word short phrase and repeat this phrase as you take slow breaths with each repetition. For 15 years I have used the phrase "I am strong." No matter what obstacles pop up, this phrase helps me to feel an immediate surge of confidence — ready to face anything!

Music: Listen to music to release the calming chemical serotonin into your body. Start singing: you get an immune boost of 240 percent.

Laugh: Laughter increases your artery diameter by 22 percent and chronic stress reduces it by 35 percent.

"E" is for exercise.

Research shows that for some people, exercise can be equal to medication in resolving depression. Exercising three times a week reduces the risk of Alzheimer's and dementia by one-third. Walking 20 minutes a day reduces your risk of death from all diseases by one-third.

New furniture: Put a treadmill or cycle in the corner of your television room. At night my husband and I burn 200–300 calories as we jump onto our treadmill and treadclimber to watch *Law and Order.* Exercising has become fun because we encourage each other!

Chair yoga: Buy a book or tape on chair yoga and do the stretches that relax and strengthen you.

Hand weight: Keep a five-pound hand weight in your bottom drawer at work or under your desk. Each lift increases your bone density.

"L" is for love.

A new study suggests that being in a cardiac rehab group reduces your risk of death by more than 50 percent. There is a strong relationship between health and community. My life became so busy at one point that my friends were squeezed out. Now I e-mail a friend every Monday, Wednesday, and Friday!

Share a meal: Make an appointment to have a meal with someone at least once or twice a week.

Join a group: Start a study or book group at work, meet for lunch, or play cards.

Get a pet: Pets reduce stress, depression, and cardiovascular disease, and boosts your immune system.

"F" is for food.

Food is medicine. Foods can help alleviate a variety of diseases and conditions including heart disease, cancer, diabetes, arthritis, obesity, insomnia and other conditions. Over the recent two decades I have discovered food is one of my greatest tools in dealing with stress and depression.

Eat breakfast: Breakfast increases your metabolism by 25 percent and stabilizes any mood swings.

Omega 3s help with depression and cardiovascular disease: Plan to eat fish three times a week or take a one-gram fish oil capsule daily.

Vitamin B-6: B-6 increases the calming hormone serotonin in your body. Take a banana to work, or eat tuna, turkey, or salmon regularly.

Blueberries: This is brain food that helps neuron reproduction and communication. It's great for mental health and antiaging.

By grounding my life in the four roots of S.E.L.F., I have regained my health, happiness, and balance. The roots have become my partners, whether I'm facing loss, failure — or even aging. Give them a try; I know they'll work for you, too.

45

Prepare the mind and the body for the decades ahead

You may have thought that the era of testing was over, but the preventative tests at this time of your life are even more important.

by Neil S. Calman, M.D.

Dr. Neil S. Calman calls himself "a flag-waving family physician" and "an urban warrior." A third-generation New Yorker, he created the Institute for Urban Family Health and has run it as a command post for training and placing family physicians and nurse practitioners in community practices all over New York City. In 2012 Dr. Calman became Professor and Chair of the Department of Family Medicine and Community Health at the Mount Sinai School of Medicine.

Sixty. Yeah! Seems to me like the perfect time to rebuild our physical and mental selves for the decades ahead. With the invulnerability of youth long gone from our psyches, we have to face the realities of our deteriorating bodies and do everything we can to preserve them. Oh, and while we are at it, it helps to reprogram some of our thought processes as well to keep our outlook optimistic and our minds sharp.

Let's start with the body. Obesity is an epidemic in the United States and if you are one of its victims, it's time to get over it! As our muscles weaken and joints start to wear out from years of use (and for some of us, abuse), the last thing we need is to be carrying around extra weight. Lose it, not by dieting but by creating a lifestyle revolution. We are what we eat, some say, and now is the time to change who we are and what we eat. The big enemies of our bodies are simple sugars (sweets, fruit juices, sodas, candy), saturated fat (animal fats, egg yellows), and highly processed foods. Buy organic. Get the pesticides and hormones out of your body by not putting more in. All of this can only help.

Exercise keeps our bodies and minds in tip-top shape. It's time to trade in the bus or car and take a fast-paced walk to get your heart pumping. Skip the elevator, walk the stairs. Pull out the old bike and get it tuned up. Think of each physical task as an opportunity to get your body going. Get yourself pumped up early in the morning with a vigorous walk and your metabolism will stay active for hours. You don't need a gym to get in shape. Buy a book of exercises. Start stretching your muscles (gently). Stretching is one of the best ways to keep your body flexible and limber, so when some reckless driver comes around the corner with two wheels off the ground, you're able to make that sudden sprint across the street with ease (and no muscle sprain).

If you're a smoker, stop. Get tough on yourself. While you cannot undo all of the cancer risk so quickly nor reverse all the damage you have done to your lungs, you can stop further deterioration in your heart, blood vessels, and lungs. Of course, you can let yourself go and start investing in a company that supplies home oxygen for your later years — but wouldn't it be smart to stop now? And if you've never smoked or have quit, insist that those around you stop blowing smoke in your face! Secondhand smoke is not some worry of overly neurotic health-nuts. It is a gaseous mixture of highly toxic gasses and particles, and prolonged or repeated exposure has been proven to be harmful. It's your life — put your foot down.

Now let's talk about medical care. There are a lot of things in medicine that we don't know, but there are some about which there is almost no controversy. The two leading causes of death from disease are still cancer and cardiovascular disease. Have you put off that colonoscopy you should have had 10 years ago? You drink some stuff, poop your brains out overnight, get an injection of an anesthetic that basically knocks you out, and when you wake up, it's all over. Wouldn't you feel totally stupid and irresponsible if your family and friends were left without you because you were afraid to get a simple test that could have saved your life?

Women need annual mammograms starting at age 40 and breast exams by a health-care provider. Those at highest risk are those with a family history of breast cancer. And don't forget cervical cancer screening. New recommendations reduce the frequency of testing to every three years if there is no history of an abnormal Pap test in the prior 10 years and if your doctor uses the new liquid-based Pao test. As an extra precaution, ask your doctor about a test for human papilloma-virus DNA which can be done during your routine gyn examination.

Testing men for prostate cancer is still optional. Many men who test positive don't have prostate cancer, and as many who test negative do have it. Still, some men and their doctors use the PSA (prostate specific antigen) as a test to see if there is any indication of cancer. The test score (whether your doctor uses 4.0 as the cutoff of normal or 2.8) and the rate at which the score has risen are both signs that a biopsy is indicated. And after the biopsy, there is much controversy as to whether treatment helps in all forms of prostate cancer and if so, which are best. You see why some men choose not to be tested?

Take care of your heart! Both men and women need to have their blood pressures and cholesterol tested to make sure that they are under control, as both are risk factors for many types of diseases of the heart and blood vessels. Get a fasting blood sugar test to make sure you don't have diabetes. I recommend some additional tests for my patients — at least once when they turn 60: a thyroid test (TSH or thyroid stimulating hormone), chemistry tests for kidney function (BUN or blood urea nitrogen and creatinine), and liver function tests (bilirubin, AST, and ALT). If you are sexually active with more than one sexual partner or with one partner who may be active with more than just you, remember that condoms are not just for teens having sex as we did in the back of the Chevy. And get an HIV test. HIV is now a chronic disease with people living long and productive lives — getting treatment with a score of new medications that are available.

So the big question: how do we keep from getting old? My father says that getting old beats the alternative. My own personal philosophy is that we have more control over how our minds and bodies age than many would like to think. You see, if you believe that things just fall apart with age and there is nothing you can do about it — well then, keep to your old evil (and unhealthy) ways and don't worry about it. If you think you can have influence on how you feel by what you do to take care of yourself, well, that puts a lot of responsibility on yourself

46

Look in the mirror

We all age, it is an inescapable truth.
We can't stop it. What we can do, however,
is change the *way* we age.

by Cap Lesesne, M.D.

Cap Lesesne, M.D., is a plastic surgeon with over 30 years of experience and is the author of *Confessions of a Park Avenue Plastic Surgeon.*

Aging is a fact of the human condition. By the time women hit 60, the effects of menopause and the decrease in estrogen have reached a plateau, and cause well-defined changes in fat deposition, i.e., saddle bags, hips and breasts, as well as in skin elasticity, tone and appearance of the skin. In men, the level of testosterone drops, which can also cause thinning of the skin and the hair, loss of skin elasticity, and predictable changes of fat deposition, i.e., a big stomach.

If you don't take care of yourself, you will age faster. The best thing you can do to slow down the aging process is to stop smoking, watch what you eat, and exercise moderately. And if, after making all these positive changes, you'd like to do a little more, you can take advantage of the medical advances now available to you: plastic surgery and routine skin maintenance.

Many developments in the medical community have increased our life spans, because diseases and complications that used to be fatal are now manageable. Initially, when penicillin was developed in the 1930s, it allowed general surgeons to perform bowel and breast surgery with a lessened risk of infection. In the 1950s, heart surgeons began to perform coronary artery bypass and heart valve replacement, and in the next decades, orthopedic surgeons and neurosurgeons began miraculous advances with artificial joints and spinal surgery.

The plastic surgeons' colleagues have helped patients to live longer, creating the opportunity for plastic surgery, which began to explode in the 1980s, to let patients live with an improved lifestyle. In the 1990s, the concept of routine skin maintenance gained worldwide acceptance. Skin maintenance involves mild, noninvasive treatments to improve the texture of your skin.

Regardless of where you live in the world, plastic surgery and routine skin maintenance are causing the concept of aging to change radically, and the demand for them to change the way a person looks is growing. If you're curious, there are guidelines to help you start on this journey if you haven't gone there before. First, remember that surgery is very good at changing contours of the face and the body, but poor at changing skin texture. You need to look at these two problems with very different solutions.

Everyone has heard about face-lifts. Not many are aware of the rapid technological changes in plastic surgery that allow for facial rejuvenation of a 60-year-old that leaves hidden, if not invisible scars. You can truly have the face you want, depending on how much effort you want to make. A plastic surgeon can restore the bone structure, subcutaneous fat, and skin distribution that was present 20 years earlier. For the body, breasts can be lifted and increased or reduced in size to make more youthful-looking breasts. Almost any place on the body can be liposuctioned and depending upon the extent of skin elasticity, legs, knees, and abdomen can be tightened, and sagging underarms corrected, as well. The possibilities are almost limitless, depending on how motivated you are.

Surgery may change the contour, but to change the texture of the skin, you may want to consider routine skin maintenance, which involves mild, noninvasive treatments. They can consist of mild chemical peels, micro dermabrasion, laser treatments, or pulse light treatments. These will make your skin smoother (in the case of some chemical peels) and, if you choose laser treatments, may increase the collagen concentration in your skin.

If you have a fine wrinkle, injectables may be the answer. The most widely used injectable is Botox. Botox stops the muscle from contracting and therefore stops the wrinkle from progressing or forming. We now know that Botox has many other uses, including reducing migraine headaches, back pain spasm, and abnormal muscle patterns of the face and neck. The beauty of Botox is that it can be used almost with impunity. The amount required for toxicity is so great that it is almost unattainable, provided the Botox is produced by a FDA-approved laboratory. Other popular fillers include Restalyne and collagen, which will help fill a wrinkle or a depression after they have formed. These resolve after several months and must be replaced. Fat grafts, using a special cleanser, are also possible and have the beauty of being nonallergenic and remaining with you for years.

To protect and maintain the skin, you should use moisturizers and/or sunblock of an SPF greater than 20. Many people aren't aware that sunblocks dissipate after more than two hours, and that you should reapply it during the day. See your dermatologist or plastic surgeon periodically to have any growths removed and to check for skin cancers which, if caught early, are usually nothing more than a nuisance.

It is a common expression for someone approaching 60 years to say, "I want to look as good as I feel." We now have the capability of making that request come true. But plastic surgery and rejuvenation are not for everyone. You have to have the right psyche, you have to have aged somewhat, and you must have some financial security. Yet for these people, we now have the capability to make them look and feel younger, opening the door for a longer life of improved appearance and self-esteem.

There are some people who overdo it. I once had a patient in her 70s who came in to have breast implants changed every six months, depending on the man she was dating. I had to stop it. I also had a man in his 70s who came in asking that his nose be altered depending on the season, thinking that it was dropping in the wintertime. Normality is somewhere in the middle of the big bell curve between narcissism and self-denial. That is true whether you are 60 or 30.

So look in the mirror. If you like what you see, don't do anything, but if in the recess of your mind, you want to look a little bit younger, or look as good as you feel inside, think about investigating plastic surgery or skin treatments.

Section Seven

THE LEADER OF THE PACK

(Shangri-Las, 1964)

47

Rediscover yourself at 60

Aging is a journey toward self-discovery
and perhaps a revolution of sorts.

by Gloria Steinem

Gloria Steinem is a writer, feminist, and social reformer. After graduating from Smith College, she went to New York City as a freelance writer, first attracting attention with her article, "I Was a Playboy Bunny", an exposé based on her own undercover work in a New York City Playboy Club. Among her many lifetime achievements, Steinem is the founder and original publisher of *Ms.* magazine.

Age is supposed to create more serenity, calm, and detachment from the world, right? Well, I'm finding just the reverse. The older I get, the more intensely I feel about the world around me, including things I once thought too small for concern; the more connected I feel to nature, though I used to prefer human invention; the more poignancy I find not only in very old people, who always got to me, but also in children; the more likely I am to feel rage when people are rendered invisible, and also to claim my own place; the more I can risk saying "no" even if "yes" means approval; and most of all, the more able I am to use my own voice, to know what I feel and say what I think; in short, to *express* without also having to *persuade.*

Some of this journey's content is uniquely mine, and I find excitement in its solitary, edge-of-the-world sensation of entering new territory with the wind whistling past my ears. Who would have imagined, for instance, that I, once among the most externalized of people, would now think of meditation as a tool of revolution (without self-authority, how can we keep standing up to external authority)? or consider inner space more important to explore than outer space? or dismay even some feminists by saying that power is also internal? or voice thoughts as contrary to everything I read in the newspapers as: The only lasting arms control is how we raise our children?

On the other hand, I know my journey's form is a common one. I'm exploring the other half of the circle — something that is especially hard in this either/or culture that tries to make us into one thing for life, and treats change as if it were a rejection of the past. Nonetheless, I see more and more people going on to a future that builds on the past but is very different from it. I see many women who spent the central years of their lives in solitary creative work or nurturing husbands and children — and some men whose work or temperament turned them inward too — who are discovering the external world of activism, politics, and tangible causes with all the same excitement that I find in understanding less tangible ones. I see many men who spent most of their lives working for external rewards, often missing their own growth as well as their children's, who are now nurturing second families, their internal lives, or both — and a few women who are following this pattern too, because they needed to do the unexpected before they could feel less than trapped by the expected.

I'm also finding a new perspective that comes from leaving the central plateau of life, and seeing more clearly the tyrannies of social expectation I've left behind. For women especially — and for men too, if they've been limited to stereotypes — we've traveled past the point when society cares very much about who we are or what we do. Most of our social value ended at fifty or so, when our youth-related powers of sexuality, childbearing, and hard work came to an end — at least, by the standards of a culture that assigns such roles — and the few powerful positions reserved for the old and wise are rarely ours anyway. Though the growing neglect and invisibility may shock and grieve us greatly at first and feel like "a period of free fall," to use Germaine Greer's phrase, it also creates a new freedom to be ourselves — without explanation. As Greer concludes in *The Change*, her book about women and aging: "The climacteric marks the end of apologizing. The chrysalis of conditioning has once and for all to break and the female woman finally to emerge."

From this new vantage point, I see that my notion of age bringing detachment was probably just one more bias designed to move some groups out of the way. If so, it's even more self-defeating than most biases — and on a much grander scale — for sooner or later, this one will catch up with all of us. Yet we've allowed a youth-centered culture to leave us so estranged from our future selves that, when asked about the years beyond fifty, sixty, or seventy — all part of the average human life span providing we can escape hunger, violence, and other epidemics — many people can see only a blank screen, or one on which they project fear of disease and dependency. This incomplete social map makes the last third of life an unknown country and leaves men stranded after their work lives are over, but it ends so much earlier for women that only a wave of noisy feminists has made us aware of its limits by going public with experiences that were once beyond its edge, from menopause as a rite of passage into what Margaret Mead called "postmenopausal zest," to the news that raised life expectancies and lowered birth rates are making older people, especially older women, a bigger share of many nations, from Europe to Japan, than ever before in history. I hope to live to the year 2030, and see what this country will be like when one in four women is sixty-five or over–as is one in five of the whole population. Perhaps we will be perennial flowers who "re-pot" ourselves and bloom in many times.

48

Discover kaizen

Kaizen is a Japanese word that means "continuous improvement." Continuous improvement is achieved only one way — by going forward.

By Linda Lopez

Linda Lopez is a co-founder and the director of the ibnMobilité program in New York. Having enjoyed successive careers in broadcasting, production, and public relations, she now draws from her extensive contacts in the New York business community to create mobilité programs for French student groups. Linda is currently an adjunct associate professor in the Media Arts department of Long Island University, where she teaches commercial and voiceover performance.

Twenty years of running has taught me a thing or two about limits. The most valuable lesson has been that, like time and the truth, they are highly subjective. On any given morning, depending on any number of variables, from what I had for breakfast to whether I feel loved, the finish line can seem either attainable or completely out of reach. This fluid state of affairs suggests I can almost always do more and better than I think I can.

At a time when many of my peers are coming to grips with a slower, creakier version of themselves, I have decided to pursue a hunch. I think the key to staying vital is to work smarter: shift gears, change strategy, rethink incentives, but do not slow down, and certainly do not stop. I have seen evidence that, with patience and persistence, a reasonably healthy person can continue to break records throughout life.

The key is in how one measures progress. At 60, I am not as fast as I was at 40, but I do have greater endurance and willpower, and I have learned a few tricks to help me stay the course. I also now know that absolutism has no place in a happy life, that any progress at all is progress just the same.

"It's a dare," my daughter used to say when, as a child, she set herself to some impossible feat. I would smile and watch her take the leap, remembering the seriousness with which I took those same self-imposed challenges when I was young. Childhood games prepare us for adult life, but I believe this particular game should be played for as long as we live, that "It's a dare" should be worn like a talisman, ready to be rubbed when we need a burst of courage or strength.

When I encounter a young gazelle in Riverside Park, my favorite place to run in New York, I get behind her, cast an imaginary string from my waist to hers, and let her pull me along. Sometimes it works and I shave a minute or two off my time; other times I end up panting and watching her disappear over the hill. But the net result is always the same: I do more than I would have on my own — and I feel the thrill of having taken the dare, of having tried.

Gentle pressure, small challenges, subtle changes, these comprise the art of kaizen, a Japanese word that expresses the way of continuous improvement. It is this approach to progress that I have embraced in the newest chapter of my life.

I walk slowly, but I never walk backward. — Abraham Lincoln

Like any good philosophy, kaizen can be applied to almost any task. In fact, good change, the literal meaning of kaizen, made its way to the West in the 1980s, not as a fix for aging athletes, but as a management tool to improve quality and process in the workplace. Companies that applied its principles reported increased profitability, lower costs, less waste, shorter lead times, improved safety, and a happier workforce.

In Kaizen: The Key to Japan's Competitive Success (McGraw-Hill, 1986), quality management consultant and kaizen pioneer Masaaki Imai laid out the principles of continuous improvement and lean manufacturing that are used today by businesses around the world.

Kaizen focuses on small changes fulfilled over time by each member of a company or team. Ideally, each change includes a behavioral component that discourages returning to the old way of doing things. This last is important because kaizen traffic moves in one direction only: forward.

In the workplace, kaizen can look something like this:

At the Haneda airport in Tokyo, an employee paints a bright yellow arrow to show in which direction the luggage carousel moves, a helpful aid for anxious travelers. At the Canon plant, a worker puts wheels on a bucket so that employees can pass parts without having to go back and forth between workstations.

Kaizen is the tiny root in the wall, growing imperceptibly, achieving ambitious ends by small and manageable steps. Like one of Suerat's pointillist paintings, it becomes more brilliant the farther away you stand. Kaizen is about the big picture. Sustained over time, it can yield results that amount to sea change.

Slow but steady wins the race. — Aesop, *The Hare and the Tortoise*

The concept of kaizen is neither new nor unique to Japanese culture. People throughout history and around the world have sung its praises, although they may have called it by other names. In contemplating this, I begin to remember any number of quotes and fables that weigh in on the subject. It leads me to wonder if anyone I know has had a kaizen experience they can share.

Rabbi Lee Friedlander happens to be an avid runner. Although he is not familiar with kaizen, my question immediately makes him think of his friend who is recovering after a long illness. He has mapped out a running program for the friend that will begin with one lap around the track and gradually accelerate as the man's strength and stamina improve. If the new regimen becomes a lifestyle, it will be kaizen.

Anna Elman was born in Chernivtsi, Ukraine, and came to America as a teenager. Trained as a classical musician, she credits music with helping her to rein in her Slavic penchant for the grand gesture. She believes she has been applying kaizen all her life without knowing it. Music, she says, must be approached one bar at a time. While talent and perfect pitch will let you grasp the music immediately, it is practice that makes a musician.

Tweak, tweak, tweak. — The perfectionist's mantra
One morning, I decide to wear one less layer than usual.

It is chilly and damp when I hit the park, and I think wistfully of down comforters and morning talk shows. "It's a dare," I remind myself. The four miles do not feel more difficult, but I know they are; my body is working harder to stay warm. I return an hour later flushed and drunk on endorphins. Life is good.

Kaizen makes my new reality easier to accommodate. Small changes over time; I can do that. Keep moving forward, set the bar a tad higher, reach a little bit farther. More love, fuller days, sounder sleep, bigger laughs, freedom to grieve, bursts of creativity, sudden adventure . . . courage to take the dare. Just like when I was young.

49

Take a running leap of faith

Bravery mixed with a little bit of foolishness just might make your dreams take flight.

by Sharon Vaughn

Sharon Vaughn started her career in music as a recording artist. After being discovered by the late Mel Tillis while singing in an Orlando club, she decided to move to Nashville, Tennessee. Sharon spent years as a session singer with such notables as Dolly Parton, Kenny Rogers, and George Jones. Her first self-penned song, "Y'all Come Back Saloon" became a breakthrough country hit with the Oak Ridge Boys on their first album. Shortly after, she wrote the iconic song, "My Heroes Have Always Been Cowboys," sung by Waylon Jennings. Willie Nelson recorded it on the Oscar®-winning soundtrack for *The Electric Horseman* and it became a number one hit. Sharon went on to write more than a hundred recorded songs, (chart topping hits by Keith Whitley-Lorrie Morgan duet, Patty Loveless, Randy Travis, and Trisha Yearwood) plus other hits sung by Martina McBride-Jimmy Buffett duet, and the "Queen of Country Music" Reba McEntire. She moved to Stockholm, Sweden where she broke into the pop realm with Agnes' worldwide hit, "Release Me" and Japan's International Song of the Year, "Rising Sun." Currently residing in Nashville and Crescent City, Florida, she continues travel to Europe composing all genres of music . . . including scores for musical theatre in Europe and the US.

Following her love of musical theatre, Vaughn composed several musicals, including *The Sweet Potato Queens*, the musical with Grammy Award–winner, Melissa Manchester and Tony Award–winner, Rupert Holmes. Their production just made a worldwide distribution deal and will be opening around the world soon.

Sharon was recently honored for her contribution to music by the Country Music Hall of Fame as a Poets and Prophets, Legendary Songwriter . . . a retrospective of her life and career . . . so far.

First Stage:

I turned sixty sitting on my dog's bed in my new residence in Port Washington, New York, she and I sharing my celebration dinner . . . a 6-inch tuna sub from Subway, a giant bag of bar-b-que potato chips and a diet coke. As grim as that sounds and unbeknownst to me, the sands of the glass were at that very moment building castles that would form the landscape of the rest of my life.

I had just moved from the safe bosom of Music City, Nashville, Tennessee, where I had built a life and career since I was in my early twenties. After twenty-three years of marriage and a parade of unsuccessful relationships, I was single and ready to jump ship from everything, including the music I loved so much. But I wasn't running from but to something new. I didn't fit anymore. Even after all the history, the hit records and successes and failures and all the years Nashville and I had shared, I didn't feel at home. I knew too much and the business was too familiar with and to me. Instinctively, I knew I needed to feel the rush of mystery again.

Second Stage:
After spending a year and a half in New York weaning myself from the security of the South, where I was born and raised, I moved again . . . to Stockholm, Sweden, birthplace of most of the pop music in the world. This was no simple jump, it was a quantum leap. I not only changed countries and cultures, I had to change my song writing style and discipline from the genre of music that had defined me all my adult life . . . from country to pop . . . immediately!

I arrived in the dead of winter, with bronchitis and knowing only two people in the entire country and neither of them very well. I could neither speak nor understand the language. So, there we were, my faithful Border Collie Bonnie and I, sitting on the floor of a minuscule rented flat in Sodermalm, Stockholm. Wiser than I, she looked at me with her jet-lagged eyes as if to say, "What the hell have you done to us this time?"

We would walk at midnight among the frozen graves in the Maria Torget Cathedral cemetery that backed up to the apartment building. Fighting despair, second guessing and the cold, I would wrap my arms around one of the massive, ancient trees that held vigil over the graveyard, place my cheek against its snowy and time-worn bark, finding comfort in its strength. "If you can become this and survive to be this, from a little tiny acorn, against all odds imaginable, I can do this!" I told it every night. I told myself every night.

Within six months of that consoling tree being imprinted on my tear-streaked soul and face, I found myself accepting the award for European Song of the Year, my first truly worldwide hit in my forty-year career. This was followed by The Japanese International Song of the Year and many, many more cuts recorded by artists all over the world.

My world expanded, my life was enriched and my vision of music, myself and the family of man was changed forever.

This Stage:
My international circle of friends is precious but a source of great frustration because I can't be all places at once to show them how much I treasure their friendship and the contribution they have made to my life. I lived in Sweden for seven years and have been traveling back and forth to Europe and the UK on a regular basis now for a decade. I have roamed the world to work with brilliant collaborators . . . to

Azerbaijan, South Africa, South Korea, Canada, the UK, Germany, Ireland, Japan, Austria, Italy, Spain, and more. I go alone, unafraid . . . alive!

At sixty, I seemed foolish and brave, maybe a little of both. It could have gone either way, I know that. But fortunately, I didn't languish there in bed, wallowing in self-pity, surrounded by empty bags of chips and the detritus of a life that needed change.

Instead, my life took a running jump off a cliff into the unknown and the fall was more like flight.

Next Stage?

50

Dream on, and achieve your goals

It's never too late to realize your dream! Your 60s can mark the start — or the accomplishment — of something big!

by Miki Gorman

Miki Gorman was born to Japanese parents in occupied China. In 1964, at the age of 28, she realized a dream when she came to the United States, then attended secretarial school, married, and had a daughter. In 1976, at 41, Ms. Gorman ran in the first five-borough New York City Marathon and won. The following year, she won again! She is the only woman to win both the Boston and New York City marathons twice, and is the first of only two woman runners to win both marathons in the same year. Gorman died from cancer at the age of 80 in Bellingham, Washington.

America is a generous country. It opened its door and accepted a powerless, non-English-speaking foreigner into its arms. I was 28 when I left Japan in 1964 on a cargo-passenger steamer bound for San Francisco. I had one suitcase and ten dollars with me.

As I watched Japan's islands sink under the horizon, I told myself I would never come back until I became established. I was afraid, but I had no regrets about the decision I had made.

On the journey across, I remembered back to the days I had spent in Tokyo. As my colleague and I walked to the subway station each evening after a long day, I often spoke to her of my hopes and dreams. Darkness fell and the streets were soon filled with neon light. I loved this short walk. During those moments, I would escape from reality and drift off into my imagination. I would picture beaches with coconut trees in the South Pacific islands, or imagine walking through cobblestone streets in Europe that I had only seen in pictures. It was the late 1950s, and women in Japan were expected to be married by their mid-20s. My friend and I were about to pass the desirable age, and everyone was looking for available bachelors. My dreams of travel, of making a better life for myself, and of becoming educated were not shared by all. There were few who had similar dreams, calling them ridiculous or nonsense, but I never stopped believing in the power of those ideas.

Finally, an opportunity came: an American couple offered to send me to school; in exchange I would be a nanny for their little boy. I attended and completed a secretarial course at Carlisle Commercial College in

Pennsylvania with the help of teachers and classmates a decade younger than I was. I found a job in Los Angeles, and shortly afterward, married an American businessman. Soon, with his encouragement, I started jogging in order to better my health. I weighed only 84 pounds then.

The initial purpose of jogging was to gain weight and improve my metabolism. I was encouraged by a friend to enter competitions, and in December 1973, at the Western Hemisphere Marathon in Culver City, California, I won the women's open division in record time. Indeed, I was surprised. I was 39 years old. "Am I the fastest woman in the world — running this distance, at least right at this moment?" I asked myself. It was an incredible feeling. I could not believe it! I trained even harder after that. I wanted to find my ultimate limit.

The peak of my running career was 1976. By then, women's races were more popular, and I had to face serious competitors. I had already given birth to my daughter, and tasted second place, and was very eager to win again. I aimed for the New York City Marathon, one of my most challenging and memorable marathon races. The night before, I was sitting alone at a corner table of the Magic Pan restaurant. While waiting to be served, I thought about my condition and training of the past year. I was confident of winning, but knew it wouldn't be easy. I had been unable to beat my strongest competitor, Kim Merritt, who was defending her title. After I was served my dinner — two full entrees of mushroom and spinach soufflé — a British couple next to me stopped their conversation and looked at me amazedly, comparing the dishes with my size. I said, "I'm running the New York City Marathon tomorrow. And I'm going to win!" Their eyes got even bigger. "Are you?" they asked, adding they would be at the finish line.

I finished first in the women's division with the time of 2 hours, 39 minutes, and 11 seconds. As promised, the British couple was there, waving enthusiastically.

Today, 30 years later, I still remember that day. I had achieved my goal. Keep your dreams in front of you and I bet that you will, too.

51

Go the distance

With training buddies and a schedule, you, too, can be a marathon runner! The mental strength you have in your 60s will make it easier for you than those half your age!

by Michael Milone, Ph.D.

Michael Milone, Ph.D, is a research psychologist in New Mexico. He has completed 33 marathons, two Ironman triathlons, and hundreds of other races, including the Mt. Taylor Winter Quadrathlon.

Don't stop reading because you think a marathon is impossible. It's not as hard as you think! Those rumors about Phedippides dying, in 490 B.C., after running 25 miles from Marathon to Athens to announce the Greek victory over the Persians, are probably untrue. Thousands of people complete a marathon each month, and most live to tell about it. And, most of them do it again.

Running a marathon in your 60s is probably easier now than when you were half that age. After six decades, we are more patient and pensive than younger runners. The ability to train for — and complete — a marathon requires far more mental strength than physical conditioning. Don't get me wrong; you've got to put in a lot of miles. It's your head that will get you there, though.

Nonrunners and runners who have not yet done a marathon overestimate the physical effort involved. I was just as guilty of this misunderstanding before I ran my first one. Although I was in great shape and regularly ran half-marathons, as well as shorter races, I had convinced myself that my knees would never hold up for 26.2 miles, and I wanted to preserve them for as long as I could.

What prompted me to undertake my first marathon was a base human instinct: competition. My wife completed a marathon before I did. What made this even more embarrassing was that my wife isn't a runner. She went to a marathon as support for a friend, who was running her first. When my wife saw the variety of people crossing the finish line — hardly the super-athletes she had envisioned, she thought, "I can do this." A year later, she completed the Flying Pig Marathon in Cincinnati, Ohio.

Realizing that I couldn't live with my wife, or myself, unless I ran a marathon, I gritted my teeth and, four months later, ran my first marathon.

It became addictive. I now try to run one a month, and do shorter races and triathlons in between. This may sound daunting, but it's not. I have friends who have run a marathon a week, for a year. Others do back-to-back races, running a marathon on Saturday and another on Sunday. For those who have completely lost their minds, there's the Labor Day Triflecta.

Now that you've started to think about doing a marathon, you should consider who your training partners are going to be. Unless you are a Zen master, you're going to need some companionship during your training, and on race day. You don't need a trainer, just some racing buddies. Perhaps you can talk some of your friends or family into it, or you can hook up with a local group. If you aren't a serious runner, don't worry. Local running groups are as interested in partying as they are in running. Sure, there are usually a few "burners" in every club but, for the most part, the members are just people who love to run. There are far more slow runners than fast ones, and the people in the back of the pack have a lot more fun than the early finishers.

A third way to find training buddies is to join a fundraising group, such as Team in Training (sponsored by the Leukemia & Lymphoma Society). TNT, as the group is called, will help you train and will support you on race day. Lots of other organizations also use marathons as fund-raisers. If you don't mind hitting up your friends and family for donations, a fund-raising group is probably the best way to prepare for and complete your first marathon. You'll meet great people, have an easier time training, and be doing an enormous amount of good through your fund-raising. In some marathons (London is the best example), the majority of the participants are raising funds, and race organizers reserve slots for these groups.

In addition to training buddies, you will need a training schedule. This will be the easiest part. There are countless books and Web sites devoted to running or walking a marathon. Scout a few of them and choose a program that matches your goals, the time you have available to train, and your personal style. If you hook up with TNT or another group, they will provide you with a training program.

Preparing for a marathon doesn't have to be intimidating. You'll have to be dedicated and consistent, but you can make it an enjoyable part of your life. Training buddies always make it easier, and music or a radio is virtually a requirement. Nothing makes the miles go by more quickly than listening to your favorite music, radio station, or book while you run or walk. Some people like to take their music or book to a marathon, but many enjoy chatting with the other participants and listening to the sounds of the crowd. Some of the most interesting people I've ever met have been running alongside me in a marathon.

This brings up the issue of the race you choose for your first marathon. Most people choose one of two options: a race that's convenient and usually local, or one that's big and spectacular. A local race is usually cheaper and more convenient, but you might end up with stretches that are pretty lonely. (That's the importance of training buddies who participate with you.) A big and spectacular race will have support throughout the course, there will always be people around you, and the crowds will provide you with the enthusiasm to get through the tough miles.

If you think that I'm guiding you toward a big race as your first marathon, you're right. In addition to the advantages I've mentioned, the big races are held in wonderful venues. The huge marathons like Chicago, Honolulu, London, New York, Paris, San Diego, or Walt Disney World are exhilarating. Everyone remembers his or her first marathon, and when the memory includes something like crossing London Tower Bridge or getting a hug from Mickey Mouse, it will bring you joy for the rest of your life!

Section Eight

I GOT YOU BABE

(Sonny & Cher, 1965)

52

Seduce someone

Prime your libido and go to bed early! Sex at 60 is fun, exciting, and can add years to your life!

by Ricardo Munarriz, M.D.

Ricardo Munarriz, M.D., an assistant professor of urology at Boston University School of Medicine, was awarded the first Bayer Urology Fellowship in Sexual Medicine. He has authored more than 80 peer-reviewed papers on male and female sexual dysfunction.

Sexagenarian: once a word you used to laugh about in high school, now a word that has you worried. Oh, you can color your hair, spruce up your wardrobe, get a few nips and tucks taken in your sagging jowls, but what can you do to start your mojo working and put some zip back in your love life?

The answer is plenty. Sure, you're not the randy 20-year-old you once were, but maybe you don't want to be. Sex when you're older — and especially if your relationship with your partner is good — can, like a ripening peach or a newly bottled wine, get better. And some of the latest research suggests that, besides relieving stress and boosting the immune system, an active sex life may actually add years to your life! So what are you waiting for? If you're having problems in bed, it's time that you cleared them up.

First of all, you should know that it's not unusual to have problems, and that they didn't happen all at once. Chalk them up to aging and lifestyle. Smoking, lifting too many martini glasses, and packing on pounds can all affect sexual function. Both sexes experience hormonal changes — men have a lessening of testosterone, while women experience low levels of estrogen. Men accumulate sports injuries. A kick to the groin playing soccer or heavy-duty bike riding can damage a man's vascular system and lead to trouble in getting, or sustaining, an erection. After 40, women often complain of pain during sex, due to a drying up of essential oils.

Some of the problems are emotional: both sexes complain of low libido. With women, it's the number one problem. It's high on the list with men also, though premature ejaculation may be their top problem.

Let's talk about men first. Please note: I'm not being sexist. It's just that until recently, most of our research has focused on men. The reason is something women have always known: they're more complex. Researchers have finally turned their attention to women, though, and I'll get to their findings in a moment.

Back to men. The first thing I tell a man with a problem is: see your primary-care physician. Have your cholesterol checked out and take a diabetes test. We know now, thanks to a study of men between the ages of 50 and 75 in Finland, that a diabetic patient is three times more likely to have sexual dysfunction than a man without diabetes.

If everything checks out, but you're still having problems, your doctor will very likely refer you to a urologist and/or a sexual-function clinic. Although our clinic has been around for more than 20 years, our phone didn't begin to ring off the hook until after March 1998, when Bob Dole and his little blue pill popped up on the TV screen.

Everyone wanted Viagra. Today, Viagra (along with Levitra and Cialis) is still what men expect to receive to cure their problems when they come to the clinic. In fact, the pill, which targets an enzyme important for maintaining an erection and is 50 to 60 percent effective, is not a cure-all. Depending on the problem — dysfunctions of libido, problems with emission/ejaculation/orgasm, impotence, and priapism — there is a variety of treatments I might recommend. These include a patch, or shots, every two or four weeks to boost low testosterone levels, a vacuum erection device reported to be 68 to 83 percent effective, penile implants, or a topical cream.

Women who dreamed of a pink Viagra to help them are, unfortunately, still dreaming. The latest tests show that Viagra is effective only with a small percentage of women who have a healthy sexual appetite. These women will sometimes experience a higher sensation with the pill. Viagra has shown no effect, though, on women with low libido.

Researchers have come up with a number of treatments to help the approximately 10 million U.S. women, ages 50 to 74, who complain of diminished sexual lubrication, pain and discomfort during intercourse, decreased arousal, and difficulty achieving orgasm. Treatments include hormones — a patch of testosterone if levels are low, or estrogen in cream or suppository form — and over-the-counter preparations, such as water-based lubricants like K-Y jelly or oil-based ones, like vegetable oils.

Both sexes have tools to help them with the physical side of sexual problems. The first line of therapy for both, however, is boosting low libido.

As we grow older, we tend to forget the little things that are really big things when it comes to maintaining a good sexual relationship.

For Men

Remember those games you used to play — surprising her with little gifts — flowers, chocolates, a book by her favorite author? Or leaving a note for her to discover when she comes home — telling her to meet you at a new restaurant, or just reminding her how much she means to you?

Chances are, you stopped playing those games because you were "too busy." You were working at a frantic pace, your eye on the future. The future that you worked so hard for is here! It's time to ease up and play those games again. You've had plenty of time to think up some new ones. And here's one tip: instead of bringing a DVD home, get active. Try telling her to meet you with a picnic lunch, and afterward, suggest a hike. You'll have an adventure, and when you come home, you can bring that happy feeling into the bedroom.

For Women

Sixty is the new 40, some people say. Remember yourself at 40? How you spent hours sometimes making yourself look good for him?

Spend some time again. Possibly you — or both of you — have been told to lose weight. So watch your diet, and his. Toss out those chips and the pints of ice cream. Have healthy snacks such as fruit, and plan low-carb meals. Dropping those pounds can also boost your love life.

As the pounds fall off, you'll want to hide those flannel pajamas. Bring out the silky lingerie, light candles, turn the lights down, play some soft music. Once you're in bed, be a good sexual communicator. Tell him frankly what you like, and how you like to be touched. And ask him what he wants. Sex, like life, is a give-and-take.

You both know each other so well; you've been through so much together. You're at ease with each other; you like each other. The bedrock for a satisfying sexual relationship is already there. It's more effective than any pill or cream. All that's left for you to do is smell the roses — and enjoy!

53

Become a parent

To be, or not to be — a parent! You may have been writing a list of pros and cons for decades, but in your 60s, it's time to get down off the fence and just do it!

by Chris Smither

Chris Smither is a singer, songwriter, and guitarist who has released 11 albums since the early '70s. His music draws deeply from the blues, American folk music, modern poets, and humanist philosophers. Mr. Smither, who wrote "Love You Like A Man," which Bonnie Raitt and Diana Krall have sung, tours nationally and internationally — performing more than 150 concerts a year at clubs, theaters, and festivals. In March 2018, Smither released his eighteenth record, Call Me Lucky.

When I was in my early 50s, I had a conversation with a Frenchwoman about children. She was married to an Englishman and living in Cornwall, with him and their three kids. And I was having vague (and sometimes not-so-vague) thoughts about having a child. I told her about my difficulty in reaching a decision.

"It's not something you decide," she said, "it's something you do."

She was speaking seriously, and she noticed that I was looking seriously puzzled. Continuing, she said, "You've spent 50-some years figuring things out, finding out what works, what doesn't, what's de la merde qui t'emmerde . . . il faut trouver le moyen de se débarrasser de ces choses."

You must find the means to unburden yourself of these things.

"En voilà trois," she said, gesturing to the kids. "There's three of them."

Eight years later, my wife and I found ourselves on a plane bound for China. On the Fourth of July, we were presented with Robin Ruoshi Smither, then ten months and two days old. We arrived home with her on Bastille Day, July 14. So much for independence and liberty.

When we were still in the consideration phase, I drew up a mental list of some of the things that militated against it. The decision to become a parent seemed formidable.

Here's what I told myself:

1. It takes a lot of energy. My sister, who had her kids when she was in her 20s, told me that it was all she could

do to keep up with them, then.

2. It takes a lot of money.

3. It's going to occupy us full-time, for what may be the rest of our lives — no respite, no empty-nest syndrome, because by the time things get that far, we'll be ready to check out.

4. No more spontaneous trips to Paris. (Well, we only did that once, anyway.) How about this: No more spontaneous trips to the drugstore, the supermarket, the movies.

5. Worry. Hostage to fortune. Stress. God, what if something happens to her? She's helpless!

There was a time in my life (not so long ago, either!) when any one of these objections would have been sufficient to shut me down.

Here is how I was able to counter all of these arguments. First, the reasonable stuff:

1. I've got less energy than I once did, but more than a lot of people half my age who are, nonetheless, pushing strollers.

2. Yes, it does cost a lot of money, but they won't give you the kid until you prove that you've got enough to raise her, one of the many ways that adoption, at least from China, differs from DIY ("Do It Yourself") parenthood.

Plus, the U.S. Government will give you a sizable tax credit to help offset initial costs.

3. Yes, it will occupy your time. Another way to look at this is that you'll never have to worry about being bored in retirement. So what were you planning to do? Shut down? Slow up? Get ready to die? This is an incentive to make sure that you live to be 100. By that time, she will be 40, which is often old enough for her to have transcended her "issues" and to have forgiven you for some of your mistakes.

4. Spontaneity is, at best, overrated. At its worst, it's a rationalization for lack of planning and the inefficient use of time. The old adage, "If you want something done, ask a busy person," never had more relevance than when applied to parents. The planning, vetting by the adoption agency, documentation, and application procedures for an adoption from China take well over a year. While we were dealing with all of that, I was acutely aware that I needed to write and collect all of the songs for my next recording before we got this kid home, knowing that I would never get it done, otherwise. By the time we got on the plane to China, I had finished exactly one song. As I write this, it has been seven months since we got home with Robin, and I am heading into the studio with a good batch of new tunes. I am astounded by how much work I can accom-

plish when I know for certain that I can count on only an hour or two a day in which to do it. The lash that I could never use on myself is wielded unconsciously and mercilessly by a half-pint.

5. Well, yes, there is a lot of worry, and there will be a lot more. It affects a lot of things in a lot of different ways. I drive differently now — more patiently, less aggressively. It doesn't matter whether or not Robin is in the car, because my own well-being is an important component of hers. There are risks involved; life is a risky business at best, and taking responsibility for another life necessarily adds to the load. This is an important point for me to consider, because, quite apart from the whole question of adopting a child, I have always tried to view and live my life as though it were an adventure. It's a conscious commitment, and the very essence of adventure is a certain amount of risk. Without risk, it ceases to be adventure and reverts to simple existence.

So much for the arguments, pro and con.

There were periods, prior to the adoption, when I was wracked by misgivings. During one of the worst of these, I called my sister to ask her advice. She told me that there was no way she could tell me what to do, but that she would like to offer an observation. "In my opinion," she said, "the inclination to do this thing — adopt this little girl — comes out of everything that is good in you, everything that makes you a valuable human being. And the disinclination to do so arises out of personal fears. No judgment, just something to consider."

She was right. We spend a lifetime learning to walk through our fears — not allowing them to rule our existence. Ultimately this is the kind of knowledge and experience that "we must unburden ourselves of." And what is the biggest fear in this case? It is that we will find love and lose it — that something will happen to the one we treasure. So, shall we deny ourselves love — even the opportunity for it — in order to protect ourselves from its loss? Some will, some won't. No judgment; just something to consider.

It's not uncommon for people to tell my wife and me, "This is such a wonderful, caring, and giving thing that you've done." It's a little ironic that, as I watch Robin toddling and prattling happily, I realize that it's the most self-centered, "me" thing I've ever done. And why not? At age 61, I'm entitled to a little self-indulgence.

54

Do what you love

Your 60s should find you winding up, not down. Step out of your comfort zone — follow your heart, nurture a baby or pet project, do what you love!

by Aleta St. James

Aleta St. James, author of *Life Shift: Let Go and Live Your Dream*, believes that impossible dreams are possible if you are willing to become the person your dream calls you to be. She also believes that beauty is power, so look as good on the outside as you feel on the inside, and know that menopause means "winding up, instead of winding down, baby." Ms. St. James became a true example of these beliefs when she delivered healthy twins at the age of 57.

At age 54, my grandmother, Nicoletta Bianchino, gave birth to my mother, the last of 13 children in an Italian-American family. My mother was the only child born in America and the jewel in my grandmother's eyes. I grew up thinking this was normal. Never once did I think it odd or far-fetched when, at the age of 49, I began to think seriously of starting my own family. My grandmother had children at a later age. Why was it strange to think that I could give birth to healthy twins at 57 and have the energy to take care of them?

Nicoletta, with her wise wisdom, inspired me with heartfelt stories of her courage and determination. She dramatically told me about her beloved father, who was one of the wealthiest men in Badi, Italy. She was brought up with servants and tutors, and was courted by many eligible suitors. Nicoletta's young heart was captured, though, when she heard my grandfather, Fidel Bianchino, serenading her with his soulful voice. One moonlit night, throwing caution to the wind, she eloped with the handsome Fidel. Her heartbroken father screamed for vengeance and called in the militia, condemning Fidel to almost certain death.

Nicoletta, who might have spent the rest of her days in a palace, hid in fear with my grandfather in a wine barrel — until she appeared three months later on her father's doorstep, armed with a marriage certificate and visibly pregnant. My grandmother, in true Puccini fashion, pleaded for her husband's life. My great-grandfather's cold heart melted, "Figlia mia (my darling daughter)," he said, "so be it." And he called off the troops.

My grandmother moved into one of the poorest houses in town, where she lived just above the chickens, with their only cow. She never looked back, and raised 12 of her 13 children there, giving birth to the last after she moved to America in 1922. I think that having this child in her 50s gave her an added zest for life that seemed to grow through her 60s, 70s, and on, along with the joy she got from each of her 20 grandchildren.

As I enter my 60s, I find myself smiling and thinking of my grandmother, while changing diapers and singing "Elmo" songs. It's true that once you have children, life will never be the same. These two little munchkins have totally detonated my fixed routine and forced me out of my comfort zone. I have now mastered the three-minute shower and the bimonthly manicure. My new mantra is: "Go With the Flow."

They have opened up my heart to experience a greater, more unselfish depth of love and brought out fierce feelings of protectiveness — as they go through their colds, high temperatures, and bumps on their heads.What am I going to do when they are teenagers and Francesca comes home with purple hair, and Gian wants to ride a motorcycle? Sometimes, I wonder how I am ever going to survive this. And then, when I think of the crazy things I did in the '60s, I wonder how my mother ever survived me! It has brought a whole different meaning to Mother's Day.

As an emotional healer and success coach over the past 25 years, I have helped thousands of people realize their deepest dreams and desires. I believe that it is never too late to live your dreams. What keeps us stuck as we get older is the fear that we don't deserve to receive what we want. We think that we are too old, too tired, or not beautiful enough to have the supportive relationship, the financial freedom, and the meaningful, joyful life we desire.

I am convinced that — just as it was in my grandmother's time — it's the enthusiasm that we have for life that keeps us going. That enthusiasm comes only from following our hearts. So many of us get bogged down in negative feelings and thoughts about ourselves that are steeped in the disappointments of the past; we stop dreaming and doing the things that really make us happy.

Having children later in life may not be what you had in mind for your 60s, but the message is still the same. Like my grandmother, Nicoletta, you must find something you love to do, and you must be passionate about it. It will fuel you with the joy and enthusiasm that will keep you winding up, not down. You are never too old to live your dreams — if you're willing to get out of your comfort zone, go with the flow, and feel like you deserve to receive what you desire.

Your desires are important; they lead you to your destiny. I'd like to leave you with this thought from my book, *Life Shift*: "No dream is too big; you just need to become the person it challenges you to be."

55

Go on a date

Faced with the possibility of reentering the dating scene? Don't worry — the scene at 60 is different, and also, you're different.

by Wendy Reid Crisp

Wendy Reid Crisp is an award-winning author whose works include three books of humor: the best-selling *100 Things I'm Not Going to Do Now That I'm Over 60; Do As I Say, Not As I Did*; and *When I Grow Up I Want To Be 60*. In 1997, she was granted an honorary doctorate from Middlebury College for her writing and speaking on behalf of women and children. She is married to John Lestina and is the mother of one son, Maximilian Crisp, and two grandsons, Cooper and Carson Crisp.

About a year after her husband of 38 years had died following a brief illness, Nancy cornered me at the church coffee hour.

"A very nice man has asked me to go places with him," she said, "and I think I'm ready. But I have some questions, and you're the only one I know who . . . "

There was a diplomatic pause. I'm the only one she knows who . . . has been married four times, twice after the age of 55. These dubious credentials have earned me the role of chief love adviser for my single, divorced, and widowed friends.

"I haven't dated since 1966," Nancy said. "That was even before the flower children, before the Summer of Love."

I told her there was no need to be nervous on that account. Unless the man is a chronic bachelor or much, much younger, the chances are that he hasn't attended too many proms in the last 40 years, either.

There are some guidelines, however; dating at 60 is not the same experience as dating at 16 — or even at 45. What's different?

Sex, for one thing — for the first thing, really, since when the subject is dating, sex is the elephant in the room. Sex is . . . different: maybe it's because women have more testosterone and men have more estrogen. Maybe it's because there are no reproductive concerns or interests. Maybe it's because mentally and spiritually we've mellowed and become more in tune with each other.

The first guideline is be aware that — whatever the reason — the mix has changed. There is as much compassion as passion, as much humility as humidity. And the ironic surprise (a serious contender in the "be careful what you wish for" category): men want to cuddle and talk.

Sometimes, not just before and after, but instead of.

Second, drop your preconceived parameters. Those of us who have found love at 60 have learned that we have had to make a few — perhaps more than a few — adjustments in our attitudes. Remember that we are no longer looking for someone with whom to build a life or have a family, so many of the characteristics we thought necessary in a good mate are no longer relevant.

For example, take college education: Who cares if a smart, skilled, interesting, and kind person has a degree? Life has either enriched us with experience or, even if we're Ivy-Leagued to the max, passed us by. Occupation is another stumbling block for some people, primarily women who consider themselves professionals and are uncomfortable at the prospect of dating, say, an electrician or a retired produce manager. (One of the happiest late-life companionships I know began over a pile of cantaloupes at Safeway.)

Also, don't cling to your biases about what pursuits you like or don't like. As the lists of yeas and nays get longer and longer, the list of potential dates gets shorter. Remember: we're seeking a companion, not a twin.

Third, look for love in all the right places. Here is a list of places where men and women I know — all over 55 — have met their late-life loves: the laundromat, church, waiting for their car to get off the lube rack, online personal ads or chat rooms, a fund-raiser for a political candidate, a bait shop, a wedding, a funeral, a grandson's college graduation, an Audubon field trip to spot osprey nests, walking a 10K run, on an airplane, college and high school reunions, a convention in Australia, the visitors' lounge at a hospital, the magazine section of a library, on a construction crew during a remodeling, an Elks Club dance (where she was dragged by friends), a bicycle repair shop, online bridge game, standing in line for a reduced-fee senior health clinic blood draw, introduction by friends, walking a field spaniel at the dog park, seated together by accident at a restaurant, forced to share a cab in a snowstorm, a tutoring session for a computer software program, in the drawer-pulls section of Home Depot.

What do these locations have in common? Attitude. With the online exceptions, these people were out of their homes and open to new experiences. They were friendly and involved in something, even if it was as simple as walking the dog or doing a load of oversized laundry. They were not afraid — not too afraid, I should say, as we are all timid to some degree — of going places alone.

Incidentally, here is some field-tested advice for women about writing ads for online dating services: list three *essential* requirements only. I found my lovely husband by winnowing down all my supposed requirements to my essential three, and I wrote: "Looking for a strong, broad-shouldered man who loves to fish." Forty-one men responded to that ad, and 39 of them were charming. Why was it so successful? The description was clear and direct, and every man knows if he fits it or not. What they aren't sure of is when subjective criteria is added, like "sensitive," "attractive," or (worst of all) "sense of humor." What does the ad writer mean? Enjoys Woody Allen or Woody Woodpecker?

Fourth, when you meet someone, take some risks. A few years ago, my uncle, Jack, called his sister, my mother, to announce that he was remarrying.

My mother said, "For heaven's sake, Jack, don't rush into anything."

Jack laughed and said, "Maxine, I'm 90. How long do you suggest I wait?"

The key to taking a risk is not if you should, but when you should. Watch for tip-off language, such as any sentence that includes the phrase "live a little" or "it's time to let loose."

Taking risks brings us to the fifth principle: Don't be afraid of making a fool of yourself. We may be sexagenarians, but when the hormones kick in, we can still be sexamorons. So what? Be a sexamoron. Your friends will forgive you and your children will welcome your return to sanity. And you may have had a splendid experience in the meantime.

Lastly, don't worry if you're on a date and when you speak, you suddenly hear the voices of your parents or your grandparents. I used to be amused (and bored) by the conversations of "old" couples, how they exclaimed over the strawberry jam — "Just like fresh strawberries, Frank!" — or the hummingbirds in the kitchen feeder. I would call my mother from the office — rushed and pressured with career, bills, kids — and ask her what she was doing. "I'm thinking about picking a cabbage for a nice soup," she'd say. Later, I knew, she and my father would discuss the soup. Should she have added the nutmeg? Was the cabbage a bit too strong?

I will not let that happen to me, I promised myself. I will never marry a man who is happy talking about the details of cabbage soup.

But I did. Thank God, I did.

Section Nine

TURN! TURN! TURN! (TO EVERYTHING THERE IS A SEASON)

(The Byrds, 1965)

56

Go fishing with your grandchildren

Captivate your grandchildren — hook, line, and sinker! It's your responsibility to teach them to fish!

by Robert E. Rich, Jr.

Robert E. Rich, Jr., president of Rich Products Corp., the largest family-owned frozen foods manufacturer in the US, based in Buffalo, New York. He is the author of *Fish Fights* and *The Fishing Club: Brothers and Sisters of the Angle.* One of three members of the South Florida Fishing Hall, he splits his fishing time between Buffalo and the Florida Keys.

Bill Dance surprised me the other day. We were chatting about out fishing lives and our families, and Dance, the Great One, the world's most recognized bass fisherman, said to me, "You know, the biggest thrill I've had in fishing is being there when all of my children, and my first grandchild, caught their first fish."

Now here's an angler who's fished and won nearly every bass tournament there is. But what he remembers most about the sport is the excitement of his grandchild's first catch.

I guess I shouldn't have been so surprised. I had just finished the manuscript of my newest book. *The Fishing Club: Brothers and Sisters of the Angle* explores the reasons why different anglers fish. During the process, I discovered that almost all of my subjects learned the sport from their grandparents — not their parents, but their grandparents!

Given the economic and time pressures on most families today, and the prevalence of two wage-earner parents per family, it makes sense that grandparents would introduce the kids to the joys of fishing.

After all, it is the grandparents who generally have more time on their hands, as well as more patience to deal with the young ones — at least over short periods of time! Dance shared with me that his grandfather, a doctor who lived in Lynchburg, Tennessee, taught him how to fish. He said he'll never forget their trips together on the river.

John Bailey, one of the most talented and prolific fish-authors in the world, also learned from a grandparent. Bailey loves to reflect on the beginning of his fishing career, when he was growing up in England. In his case, it was his grandmother who took him to a lake and fastened a bobber to his line. After awhile, the bobber went down, thrilling him! He'd snared his first fish! With his grandmother cheering him on, Bailey reeled in his line — revealing a fish cleverly disguised as a large green turtle. Bailey has fond memories of this experience. It helped him to know his grandmother better, he said.

One of my pals, Scott Keller, a trout guide out West, smiles when he talks about how his grandfather taught him to fish in California. The two went out on a small lake in a little boat. After they anchored up, Keller's grandfather took out a pound of cheese and showed his young grandson how to roll small cheese balls that they then tossed into the water.

After about five minutes, which probably seemed like an eternity to Keller at this young age, his grandfather hooked a cheese ball to his line. Not surprisingly, Keller caught his first fish. "He showed me right then how to 'match the hatch,' " Keller told me, smiling. "I decided that day that not only did I love to fish, but that I wanted to be a fishing guide."

Even President George H. W. Bush remembers learning how to fish from his grandfather, off the coast of Maine. "His boat was called *Tomboy*," he recalls, "and sometimes when I got older, he'd let me drive. I guess that's where I got my love of the ocean and fishing and boats." Are you surprised that this very busy man, during his tenure as probably the most powerful man on Earth, still made time to fish? I'm not.

Lastly, there's William Bradley, one of the most interesting people I've met while fishing. An older gentleman, Bradley fishes every day in the summer from his favorite pier in my hometown, Buffalo, New York. Mr. Bradley's ancestors were slaves in South Carolina, where he grew up. A twinkle came to his eye when he talked about his grandfather waking him up early to go fishing.

"Is that because that's when the fish bit the best?" I asked him.

"Not actually," he replied. "He just liked to get up and sneak out early, so he didn't have to work in those cotton fields."

And then Bradley said something that echoed a feeling that I have. "My grandfather was a wonderful man," he said, "and I'll never forget him. I want to teach my grandchildren to fish just like he taught me."

There is a great deal of precedent in literature for the old to teach the young to fish. In his novel *The Old Man and the Sea*, for example, Ernest Hemingway penned a loving relationship between the old fisherman, Santiago, and the five-year-old boy, Manolin, he took out fishing with him. My favorite lines from this novel read:

> Everything about him was old except his eyes and they were the same color as the sea and were cheerful and undefeated . . . the old man had taught the boy to fish and the boy loved him.

As I reflected on this one night, getting ready for bed and feeling a bit "long of tooth," I thought of my seven young grandkids, and how pleased I was that many of them would be old enough to go fishing with me this summer.

Then a cold thought entered my mind and went right to my gut. It was quickly followed by thoughts even more painful. Maybe my grandchildren won't remember the experience, or maybe it will become a blur. Maybe I'll become irrelevant. Or worse, after I'm gone, maybe they won't remember me.

Thumbing again through *The Old Man and the Sea,* I came across a conversation between the old man and the boy about their first fishing trip together:

> "Can you really remember or did I just tell it to you?"
>
> "I remember everything from when we first went together." The old man looked at him with his sun-burned, confident loving eyes.

That's it, I thought, as I got into bed and turned out the lights. Seven new anglers are going fishing with their grandpa this summer. Isn't it ironic that grandchildren, whose births at first make us feel so very old, can suddenly make us feel young again — through the student/teacher dynamic — as we quest for fish?

At the end of the day, fishing may not provide us with immortality. But it will give us a chance to pass along a pastime/sport to our grandkids, and provide them with memories they'll never forget. Some of those memories will be of us.

Sixty things to do when you turn 60: One of them should be to take your grandchildren fishing.

57

Dance with the farmer who grows your food

Farmers' markets provide fresh, locally grown produce and create a community of friends, too. So grab a partner, put on your dancing shoes, and celebrate the harvest.

By Gwen Roland

In May 1972, Gwen Carpenter left word for her M.S. diploma to be mailed in care of the Bayou Sorrell Trading Post. For nearly a decade after that, she lived in a houseboat in the middle of Louisiana's Atchafalaya Swamp. Her journal from those days of living off the land and water was published in the book *Atchafalaya Houseboat.* Gwen continued to write about food and farming for the Southern Region Sustainable Agriculture Research and Education Program based at the University of Georgia-Griffin Campus until retiring in 2010. Today she lives with her husband in Pike County, Georgia, and raises much of their food with the help of horse manure, chickens, honeybees and earthworms.

One reason I went to the swamp was to have more control over my food supply. Other reasons concerned a bearded swamper with startling blue eyes, but that's for another book. At that time agriculture was headed toward a better-farming-through-chemicals mode that depended on synthetic fertilizer, insecticides, and herbicides as well as diesel fuel to haul them all over the country. Also part of the game plan was the notion that a handful of states could feed the rest of the nation. Transporting food 2,000 miles from farm to fork was something to brag about, and long-distance truckers were the heroes of country songs. Only a few people were beginning to suspect that Merle Haggard's *White Line Fever* might be as much about the food as it was about the trucker who hauled it.

While protests about war and women's rights were getting all the headlines, the counterculture also had a gentler side. Student kitchens from coast to coast were turning out culinary acts of revolution that included whole grains seasoned with herbs and salad greens raised in window boxes. We sought out varieties that were bred for taste rather than shipping qualities to plant in kitchen gardens behind dorms and apartments.

As we went out into the world, some of us kept going, looking for self-sufficiency or creative inspiration or just a whale of a good adventure. Others settled down right away and started raising families. But as we dispersed, the love for really good food — grown locally and eaten fresh — remained a common denominator.

In those days, good food had to be homegrown since there was no infrastructure for local food systems. For me that included catching catfish in early summer to fry up crispy brown, served alongside sweet corn on the cob and tomatoes. Or later in the summer harvesting blue crabs and smothering them down in a roux with fresh okra to serve over a bed of rice. During the high-water months I added crawfish to everything from etouffee to omelets. Come winter it was wild ducks cooked with turnips from the fall garden.

One of the biggest shocks about returning to civilization nearly a decade later (a lifestyle change that concerned a handsome riverboat engineer, but that's for the other book) was having to eat long-hauled food from grocery store chains. When I went to the swamp in the early '70s there were fewer than 200 farmers' markets in the entire country. When I came out of the swamp. local food options had increased a bit on both coasts but not in the South where I lived. I planted a few hills of produce in backyards wherever I happened to be living and looked for other gardeners to swap with. It was a hit-or-miss situation.

However, other foodies were networking the same way, and eventually a movement took shape as those back-to-the-earth gardeners matured into the pioneers of organic farming and local food systems. Today, community gardens thrive in school yards and on city rooftops. At least 3,000 farmers' markets provide a place to exchange local food for local dollars.

The most important local food connection for me is Market on the Square in Pike County, Georgia. I was part of a small group of consumers who started the market in 2002 because we wanted a place to buy local food. Naysayers predicted failure since agriculture supposedly was long gone from our rural county — everyone leaves his or her country home in the morning to work in nearby cities. But it was what these country-dwelling urban workers did on their off hours that fooled the pessimists. They were gardening, often overwhelming their families and close friends with the extra produce.

The local bank donated use of a pecan grove across the street from the courthouse, so we called our fledgling group Market on the Square. Now hobby gardeners had a place to sell that seasonal abundance, lugging it to market in new SUVs and old pickup trucks, sometimes the odd Honda Civic piled to the headliner with collards. Perennials got into the act as blueberries that had gone untended for years had a reason to be pruned, watered, and picked. The budding entrepreneurs even started making use of those multiplying lilies along the driveway or the bee balm taking over the flower bed.

During the peak season as many as 35 vendors circle the pecan grove with tables and tailgates loaded down for our convenient shopping. The growers have educated their customers about marauding raccoons, drought, and why they can't expect local sweet corn and strawberries at the same time. Both sides also have learned that good food costs good money, so now our growers not only get the satisfaction of seeing their crops in demand, but they make decent money on the sales.

Another unexpected bonus of our farmers' market is the sense of community that has developed during Saturday mornings under the pecan trees. It's the only place during the week that county residents of all ages and races meet as neighbors. We exchange recipes, get free blood pressure checks, listen to a storyteller, watch a whittler.

Some of the market regulars also meet on the first Saturday of every month to dance to old-time music. Singles, couples, and entire families come to the Birdie Community Clubhouse that has withstood more than 50 years of shuffling feet. The high point of the market season is the day our dance group performs at the market. If we are lucky, some local musicians saw out an old hoedown. If not, we hook up a battery tape player and swing into Virginia reel or another old dance so easy that the line between audience and performers blurs and then disappears. We grab partners from the sidelines and whirl under the canopy of leaves.

Sixty is a great time to get in touch with your community by dancing with the farmer who grows your food. If your community doesn't yet have a farmers' market or an old-time dance group, 60 is the perfect age to start one.

58

Put yourself first

As you hit the big 6-0, it's time to finally put yourself first. You've earned the right to be a little selfish!

by Jules R. Altfas, M.D.

Jules R. Altfas, M.D., practices psychiatry in Portland, Oregon, specializing in clinical work with Attention Deficit Hyperactivity Disorder (ADHD) adults. He is a pioneer in the study of connections between ADHD and obesity. Dr. Altfas is also an avid printmaker and photographer, and has work displayed in local galleries.

Practicing psychiatry for 32 years has taught me a lot about human nature, and the best teachers have been my patients. Their experiences — in the course of struggling with myriad conditions — have shed a lot of light on what it takes to surpass life's benchmarks. It seems right to pass along a few of the lessons I've learned.

Sixty is a crucial age; it is literally the crossroads at which you decide to go one way or another — where you choose a direction or path for the remainder of the journey. At 60, many of us are still healthy, energetic, ambitious, and smart. A 60-year-old will often feel "not a day over 40"; possibility still beckons. Even so, reality is quietly prodding us to get going.

Turning 60 can have a downside. The physician in me is naturally drawn to concerns about health, given that in the later decades of life, health problems, since they tend to be cumulative, frequently become more prominent. Taking care of one's health belongs among the top items on the "to do" list. Everyone knows the drill: quit smoking, change your diet, exercise.

If you've been putting it off, and your internist hasn't bugged you enough already, it's important to have a screening colonoscopy. It's really not so terrible, and I have two friends whose lives were saved by it. Please make the appointment.

What is often harder is accomplishing the task we could call "maturing," or maybe better, "realizing a self" and having a sense of purpose, or direction. This is not a mere philosophical exercise, but rather a practical consideration of how to do what is best for oneself and others.

Patients commonly describe for me how they have spent their entire lives thinking about and taking care of other people, jobs, dogs, cars — everything and everyone but themselves. They could and did solve others' problems, looked after others' needs, but did not attend to their own.

Now, at 60, it often happens that they become and feel less "needed" — their kids are grown, their jobs are no longer challenging, and there's nothing left to fix. Individuals with this trouble often vastly underestimate themselves. They dwell on their failings, but don't at all remember their actions, which produced successes. It makes it hard to achieve goals, or really even to have goals. Essentially drifting, they can't use their gifts and talents to full advantage, which is tragic for them, and deprives all of us of their potential contributions.

In the worst instance, a person in this state becomes depressed, among the most common of human ailments, or some other condition that is equally debilitating. At this point, treatment is a necessity and must not be neglected.

Most 60-year-olds won't be so gravely affected, but are likely to have at least a hint of such experiences. Remember, it's normal to stop at any age and take the time to ask oneself: What is important? After all, growing and learning are pleasurable and enriching throughout our lives, and according to experts, they are what keeps the brain limber.

Okay, you want to know what to do. Be forewarned: it's not for the faint of heart. But here it is: finish the job of becoming you. Summon the courage to notice your successes; then, take them to heart and learn from them. The result is that you will trust yourself, rely on your own view of reality, and not have to depend on the feedback of others to value what you have done.

So, how is this achieved? Here's the recipe: Whatever you do, first make sure it is good for you. Second, be certain that there is something worthwhile that you get out of it. And third, extract a reward while achieving it.

I know it sounds "selfish." But just think a moment. How can it mean anything if you hold back and don't put yourself into it? If you get nothing out of it, you'll have no feeling for it — for you'll have no investment in it. It's true both ways — put nothing in, you'll get nothing out; get nothing from it, and there's nothing to put into it.

Distilled to its essence, the lesson is: "Do what is really best for you, and it will be good for others, as well." So far, this lesson has never been disproved. Find the courage to value what you do right, not just what you do wrong, and have a self to share and to receive.

That's all there is to it. Have fun when you turn 60. 

59

Hit the road

Time is wasting! At 60, this is not a dress rehearsal! Follow your dream, satisfy your wanderlust, travel the world!

by Alan Lewis

Alan Lewis is the chairman of Kensington Investment Company and chairman and CEO of the Boston-based Grand Circle Corporation, America's leading provider of international travel, adventure, and discovery for Americans over 50; and the parent company of Grand Circle Travel, Grand Circle Cruise Line, and Overseas Adventure Travel.

The poet Langston Hughes penned, "What happens to a dream deferred? Does it dry up like a raisin in the sun?" I hope never to discover what happens, because I don't intend to put off my dreams one single day longer. And neither should you. Let's face it: When you reach your 60s, "carpe diem" comes with a disclaimer that the quantity of available days for seizing is limited — but not the quality. Once you embrace that concept, it can be just the excuse you need to stop the daydreaming and start doing.

Those dreams often involve travel. Americans over 50 consistently identify travel as the number one pastime they hope to pursue after retirement. A *Modern Maturity* survey showed that mature Americans traveled three-plus times a year, more than any other age group. And why shouldn't we? We represent the healthiest, wealthiest, best-educated, and most leisure-oriented senior generation in history. We will never be in a better position to enjoy these gifts. The legendary ski-film director Warren Miller had it right when he said, "Go this year, otherwise you'll just be another year older when you do go."

Go as far as you can

Perhaps, in the past, you had constraints that limited your geographic reach. Time, money, children, work — all the factors that made the "two-weeks-at-the-beach" or "midwinter Florida getaway" variety so popular. I have many happy memories of those trips. Why not push the envelope a bit, though? If you've vacationed at the same place every summer for the past 40 years, try something completely different.

So, where to start? Pick up a catalog from a reputable tour operator, and you'll see that there are no limits, regardless of age. Exploring Tibet? The Amazon? A Botswana safari? No problem. Experiences that were once limited to the rich (or ridiculously rugged) are now affordably and safely within your reach. Don't be daunted by distance or logistics. With the right travel operator, it will be easy as pie. Once you've done it, the sense of accomplishment, empowerment, and enrichment will inspire you to go again — and again and again.

Go with a good group

Let's dispel a myth: you needn't surrender your independence to enjoy a group tour. Nor do you have to be herded around at whirlwind speed. Group tours are no longer the same old If-It's-Tuesday-This-Must-Be-Belgium jaunts that gave them a (deserved) bad name. A good group tour will offer the ultimate in convenience and value, while still honoring your individuality — and because they "buy in bulk," they'll offer prices you could never match on your own. When you shop around, don't just compare prices; compare the features that are included for that price. Are most meals covered? What about sightseeing and admissions? Are there hidden taxes or service charges? A reputable company will tell you exactly what is, and what is not, "extra" right up front.

Let's not forget that "time is money." With all the planning and logistics taken care of, you will be free to make the most of every minute, and do what you came to do: enjoy. So, look for itineraries with pacing that is not breakneck, with longer stays in the places that matter most.

Go your own way

Maybe you always traveled with a spouse, but are now alone. Maybe your wife's health prevents her from joining activities you'd like to pursue. Perhaps your travel pal isn't available when you want to go. None of this needs to be a barrier. Check your church newsletter, personal ads, professional and civic groups, garden club, gym, senior center, alumni association — you're likely to find a willing and able travel partner.

Going solo is a more viable option than ever, especially on group tours. First, there's the built-in camaraderie. With new friends and your tour guide there to take care of you, you'll feel safe and secure as you chart new horizons. Many companies will try to match you with a roommate, so you can avoid the single supplement that hotels and cruise lines often charge. And, there's the distinct possibility that you'll meet a lifetime friend and future travel partner.

Go open-minded

Look beyond the headlines. Leave your prejudices at home. Go beyond the tourist attractions. Be open to people, to life — in all its crazy varieties. Travel is all about attitude. If you stay open-minded and positive, I guarantee that you will be rewarded.

You'll get the most out of your trip if you can connect with the authentic culture and learn something. People all over the world really do like Americans. They may not like our politics, but as a people, we are typically perceived as friendly, generous, and warm. If you don't have an overseas friend to help with introductions, a skillful tour guide can work wonders. He or she will be your entrée to the host culture, and his or her insider knowledge, local connections, and energy can make or break a trip.

The makeup of your group is also critical. Smaller groups offer a more intimate feel and the best possibilities for an incisive, authentic look at the culture. You can get close to daily life, try on local customs, and see and do things that are simply not possible in a crowd.

Go for the unexpected

My wife, Harriet, and I travel constantly, and our fondest memories are of unexpected encounters. Once, we went to climb Mt. Kilimanjaro, in Tanzania, and Harriet got sick. So, we visited the nearest Masaai village, instead. Here, we met the village chief, Kipulolo, and his warrior, Lamanyani. We talked about everything, and discovered that as human beings, we had far more in common than we thought. Still, the places we called home were vastly different. Since the chief had never ventured beyond his village, we invited him to be our guest, in Boston.

This trip changed people's lives on both sides of the world. I can't tell you what a thrill it was for the chief and Lamanyani to set foot on a plane, to ride up to the top of a skyscraper, to visit an American school. I can't tell you what an eye-opener it was for Bostonians to see him walking down Newbury Street in his crimson Maasai robes. I can't tell you how inspiring it was for our associates to hear him address a crowd of 500, and make us feel his concern for the health and education of his village's children.

I can tell you that when Chief Kipulolo told his tribe that he was thinking of traveling to Boston, a dozen voices piped up: "It's too far!" "Too dangerous!" "No one has ever gone there." "It's calving season." "You are too old."

Thankfully, he listened to the one voice, deep inside him, that said, "Just go. Go now."

60

Build a natural legacy

As you reach the age of 60, opportunities abound to leave a legacy of riches that is available to everyone — the natural world!

By Steve McCormick

Steve McCormick is the president and CEO of The Nature Conservancy. Steve is currently a Special Advisor at the David and Lucille Packard Foundation. He is also a co-founder of the Earth Genome Project, a start-up venture to create the first global, open-source database on ecosystem services and natural capital, designed to guide decision-makers in the private and public sectors. Steve and his wife Kathryn have two daughters, Kelly and Hannah.

Turning 60 is a time to contemplate leaving a legacy, something that can be achieved in a myriad of ways. I can think of few legacies more important or more enduring than leaving the natural world a little better off and thriving with life.

By exploring nature's wonders, cultivating a love for the natural world in younger generations and investing in the Earth's future, you will enrich your own quality of life while also preserving our rich natural heritage for others. Your actions today will ensure that the places you love, and even places that you never had the opportunity to know, will be around for future generations of people to discover and come to love for themselves.

For a lifetime of air you have breathed, the clean water you have drunk, and the natural beauty that has inspired wonder and awe . . . why not give something back?

Indulge

If the natural world figured prominently in your first 59 years, turning 60 is a good time to honor it . . . or make up for lost time if it has not. Embark on the natural holiday you have always dreamed about. Raft through the Grand Canyon. Hike the Inca Trail. Sail Indonesia's Spice Islands. Cruise down the Amazon. Marvel at California's redwoods. Explore the real *Shangri-la* in China's breathtaking Yunnan Province.

Ecotours that are sensitive to the fragile balance of nature offer a wonderful opportunity to learn about and understand new places and new cultures. They are also a great way to support both conservation and the local communities dependent on these natural areas.

In your own neighborhood, find sanctuary in your community open spaces. Explore the natural mysteries hiding just outside your door in your local parks. Take your camera and capture the splendor of a grove of trees or the delicate petals of a flower. Conservation groups have made great strides over the last decades converting railroad beds and industrial roads into walking and biking paths. As busy lives continue well beyond 60 years these days, local escapes can bring the beauty of nature into your everyday world.

In your own gardens and patios, look for native plants and flowers to indulge your senses. Native species are highly adapted to your unique climate and environment, require less maintenance than nonnative plants and offer year-round delight. Ask your garden shop to help you incorporate native plants into your landscape. Let your 60s be a time to revel in nature.

Inspire

Take your grandchildren or other young family members on some of these adventures. Instill in the next generation an appreciation of the outdoors and a love of nature. Take them to see bison in the wild or the annual migration of sandhill cranes in America's Midwest. Go camping, hiking, canoeing, or bicycling. And if it is within your means, give them the very special treat of seeing Komodo dragons, African elephants, or rainforest sloths in their natural habitat. Acquaint them with the indigenous people who live and work among these awe-inspiring creatures and landscapes. Better still, take a conservation vacation with your family — one that lets you volunteer. Build a bond with your loved ones as you help with environmental research projects or remove invasive species while restoring native plants. These activities will bring you closer together as you nurture the places and habitats critical to preserving the functional balance and beauty of our planet.

Closer to home, you can get involved in conservation at a community level. There are preservation groups, scout troops, and cleanup committees throughout your neighborhood that need the support of caring citizens. When you actively engage in protecting your own natural world, you support a culture of activism and personal responsibility that can become a powerful legacy for your family and your community.

Within your own household, look for ways to conserve natural resources. Leading by example can inspire others to share your concern. There are several simple steps you can take to reduce your "environmental footprint." Use and reuse cloth grocery bags instead of plastic or paper. Participate in your community's recycling program by regularly recycling your glass, plastic, and aluminum containers. Repair leaking and dripping faucets and toilets quickly. If you are planning improvements to your home, look for building products that incorporate recycled materials or timber that is certified as being produced legally. Choose high-insulating windows and doors and environmentally friendly lightbulbs. These simple actions will reduce your family's impact on the environment and encourage corporations to continue to develop new environmentally responsible products.

Invest

Keeping the natural world healthy and intact is a shared responsibility. It takes commitment from both the public and the private sectors. Another valued way to build a natural legacy is to include nature in your estate planning. As the head of a conservation organization dependent on private donations, I am continually appreciative of and inspired by those who honor nature through their financial generosity.

Whether you give $10 or $10 million to conservation, every penny helps protect the places important to you and your family. Whether it be the sweeping grasslands of Minnesota or the vibrant coral reefs of Papua New Guinea; the towering mountains of Colorado or the grand rivers of China — there is a special place in the world that touches each of us.

Find an organization that you trust, and request information on how you can become involved in its mission. Most groups can develop a plan of giving that best suits your needs. By working with conservation nonprofits now, you can guarantee that your legacy will serve nature long after she has reclaimed you.

About the Editors

Andrea Feld, GENERAL EDITOR, is a writer and editor in New York City. She is the former managing editor of *Bride's* magazine, where she also held the positions of copy and features editor and features editor, and edited 11 books in the wedding planning and entertainment areas. She began her career at *Politicks & Other Human Interests* and at McGraw-Hill, on the staff of *Today's Secretary.* As the online project director of The Foundation Center, she edited *Philanthropy News Digest,* and most recently was the editor of the *Hampton Sheet.* She has contributed essays to the book *Heroines: Remarkable & Inspiring Women* and articles to *Parenting, Sesame Street Parents, New York Newsday, Newsday's Guide to Your Dream Ceremony and Reception, Wedding Trends & News, Wedding Dresses, The Home News, The Asbury Park Sunday Press,* and the *Smith Alumnae Quarterly.*

Sheri Bell-Rehwoldt, COMMISSIONING EDITOR, is an award-winning freelance writer and editor who has penned profiles, travel pieces, and offbeat features for Web sites and publications including *American Profile, Family Circle, Go, Ladies' Home Journal,* and *The Washington Post.* She is a member of the American Society of Journalists and Authors (ASJA) and the Society of Children's Book Writers & Illustrators (SCBWI). In July 2006, Nomad Press published her activity book for children, *Great World War II Projects You Can Build Yourself,* and in January 2007 will publish *Amazing*

Maya Inventions You Can Build Yourself. Chronicle Books will publish Sheri's first picture book, *You Think It's Easy Being the Tooth Fairy?*, in 2007. Other news is available at her Web site: www.Bell-Rehwoldt.com.

Joy Darlington, COMMISSIONING EDITOR, is a journalist, novelist, and editor in New York City. Her novels include *Fast Friends* (Doubleday) and *Those Van der Meer Women* (Putnam). She has been an investigative reporter and a freelance health and lifestyle writer and editor. Her work has appeared in *The New York Times, Newsday, Readers Digest, Good Housekeeping,* and *Woman's Day.*

Bruce Fraser, COMMISSIONING EDITOR, is an award-winning financial writer and editor based in New York City. He has contributed to *The New York Times,* the *Christian Science Monitor,* CNBC.com, Forbes.com, *Wealth Manager, Financial Advisor, Crain's New York Business,* and *Nation's Business.* He has also written and edited *The Treasury Manager* and *AMEX Special Situations* newsletters. Fraser taught at Baruch College (CUNY) and Pace University. He is a member of the American Society of Journalists and Authors (ASJA), the New York Financial Writers' Association, and Editorial Freelancers Association (EFA). He is working on a book about inheritances.

Acknowledgments

I'd like to acknowledge the authors of the essays, who willingly submitted to several rounds of edits without complaining and who volunteered so much of their time and effort.

Andrea Feld

Many warm thanks to the lovely essayists who contributed their wit and wisdom to this book. I was struck by their passion, vision, grace, and humor. I can honestly say I am a better person for having been involved in this project, and send my best wishes (and gratitude) to everyone who was brave enough to put their thoughts to paper. And many thanks to Lizzie Stewart, my editor at Ronnie Sellers Productions. You were a joy to work with.

Sheri Bell-Rehwoldt

I'd like to thank all the doctors and other top-ranking professionals who wrote such lively essays and submitted cheerfully to several rounds of edits.

Joy Darlington

I'd like to thank the essayists who contributed their time and energies to bringing to fruition this book. All are at the apex of their profession. Special thanks to Rubenstein Associates Inc. for their invaluable assistance. I'd also like to acknowledge my partner, Beryl Goldberg, and Janice Fioravante for their help in editing the business and financial management sections of this book.

Bruce Fraser

Credits: continued from copyright page

Never, ever give up © 2018 Diana Nyad, Originally published as *"Never, Ever Give Up,"* in *The Singju Post Staff,* November 29, 2014; *Take off your clothes* © 2006 Cynthia Thayer; *Let it go* © 2006 Daniel J. Benor, M.D.; *It's not too late to be what you might have been* © 2006 Alison Teal; *Question everything* © 2006 Leo Sewell; *Go directly to jail* © 2006 Kathy J. Marshack, Ph.D., P.S.; *Do unto others* © 2006 Gerald S. Migdol; *Follow your passions* © 2006 Seawell J. Brandau; *Make a difference* © 2006 Suzanne Wright; *Find your island* © 2006 Jamie Wyeth; *Dare to believe in ghosts* © 2006 Mark Nesbitt; *Be a saint* © 2006 Father James Martin; *Set your intention* © 2006 Catherine Shainberg, Ph.D.; *Pray* © 2006 Leslie Williams, Ph.D.; *Reflections on turning 60* © 2006 Rev. Kenneth W. Collier; *Go to where the art is* © 2006 Faith Ringgold; *Keep your sense of humor* © 2006 Judy Brown; *Go ahead and inhale* © 2006 Alice Waldman; *Ask the big questions* © 2006 Tina B. Tessina, Ph.D.; *Chill out and meditate* © 2006 Joan Goldstein; *Leave a legacy of care* © 2006 Mary Pearl; *Be inspired night and day* © 2006 Greg Mort; *Fall in love* © 2006 Fran Maher and Brian Coffey; *Live to 100!* © 2006 Thomas Perls, M.D.; *Learn new tricks* © 2006 Mel Boring; *Rejuvenate your mind* © 2006 Roger K. Pitman, M.D.; *Live like a kid* © 2006 Frank J. Miele; *Get rich quick* © 2006 Loral Langemeier; *Start a business* © 2006 Virgil Scudder; *Make a commitment* © 2006 Laura Schatzberg; *Discover what matters* © 2006 Judith E. Glaser; *Milk your cash cow* © 2006 Jeff Harris, Ch.F.C.; *Budget for 100 years* © 2006 Anna M. Rappaport, F.S.A.; *Buy and hold* © 2006 Nick Murray; *Use some will power* © 2006 Sanford J. Schlesinger, Esq.; *Rethink your insurance strategy* © 2006 Richard Bailey; *Get your 100,000-mile tune-up* © 2006 Evan Appelbaum, M.D.; *Get physical* © 2006 Edward G. McFarland, M.D.; *Treat yourself like a star* © 2006 Nicholas V. Perricone, M.D.; *Cherish every day* © 2006 Mellanie True Hills; *Be a mover and a shaker* © 2006 Charles Faulkner Bryan, Jr.; *Sleep tight* © 2006 Gerard Lombardo, M.D.; *Be comprehensive with your health* © 2006 Jacob Teitelbaum, M.D.; *Stress: the good, the bad, the ugly* © 2006 Dr. Kathleen Hall, Ph.D.; *Prepare the mind and body for the decades ahead* © 2006 Neil S. Calman, M.D.; *Look in the mirror* © 2006 Cap Lesesne, M.D.; *Rediscover yourself at 60* © 2006 Gloria Steinem; *Discover kaizen* © 2006 Linda Lopez; *Take a running leap of faith* © 2018 Sharon Vaughn; *Dream on, and achieve your goals* © 2006 Miki Gorman; *Go the distance* © 2006 Michael Milone, Ph.D.; *Seduce someone* © 2006 Ricardo Munarriz, M.D.; *Become a parent* © 2006 Chris Smither; *Do what you love* © 2006 Aleta St. James; *Go on a date* © 2006 Wendy Reid Crisp; *Go fishing with your grandchildren* © 2006 Robert E. Rich, Jr.; *Dance with the farmer who grows your food* © 2006 Gwen Roland; *Put yourself first* © 2006 Jules R. Altfas, M.D.; *Hit the road* © 2006 Alan Lewis; *Build a natural legacy* © 2006 Steve McCormick